FORGIVING A PERFECT GOD
Resolving Anger with Divinity

FORGIVING A PERFECT GOD

Resolving Anger with Divinity

La Tonya M. Daniels

Priceless Advisor

ISBN 979-8-9863554-0-5 (Paperback)

Book production and cover design by Priceless Advisor Publishing
Interior layout and design by Priceless Advisor Publishing

Published in Las Vegas, Nevada by Priceless Advisor Publishing.
Email: pricelessadvisor@gmail.com
Website: pricelessadvisor.org

This book is dedicated to two of my best friends who are now hanging out with my Best Friend, Jesus. Charlotte and Erin thank you for your encouragement, tough love, listening ear, moments of laughter and shared tears. I miss you both and I am eternally grateful for your friendship.

Table of Contents

Acknowledgements

I would like to thank the several people for their support and love throughout this entire process. I thank God for Pastor Naida M. Parson, PhD for her insistence that I begin to write about the impasse I had with God. She was the catalyst for the documentation of this journey. She and the New Antioch Christian Fellowship stood by me and was the church I truly needed.

My heart is full of gratitude for Crystal Daniels. She did so much more than edit this book. Without her presence and her love, I would never have made it this far. I want to thank her for taking care of her big sister. I praise God for Raejon Manuel for being that friend who listened and shared as I struggled through this journey. She was often a voice of reason while being understanding and I know she was placed in my life for this very reason.

Many thanks to Rekesha Pittman for her guidance and her classes. I may not have completed them, but I've completed this book—finally. I am truly grateful for the prophetic words given to me by Pastor Antone Dotson-Parson and Del Shana Moore. Chapter six exists because of Pastor Antone's word to me, and the blood is no longer on my hands because of Del Shana's encouragement.

I'm grateful for Liv Dooley, Jamila Eddins and Valorie Williams for providing the necessary tools I needed to become an indie author. All of them helped without hesitation and with a cheerful heart.

Last, but certainly not least, I want to show my appreciation to my "Fairy Godmother", Lois Greene. Her investment in me and her diligence in seeing that I do business right has been a true blessing from our gracious Heavenly Father.

God has given each of you a gift from
his great variety of spiritual gifts.
Use them well to serve one another.
(1 Peter 4:10 NLT)

Introduction

Yes, it is taboo to be angry with God, especially if you are a Christian. Though the world tends to blame God for all its tragedy, He is not the cause. Mankind brought sin into this world and sin is the root cause of all its issues. That doesn't mean people can't sometimes misplace their anger and feel angry with what God has allowed into their lives. I certainly did. I was angry enough to shut down completely and lose sight of who I was and what I was called to do. I found that I didn't have a clue as to how to forgive Someone I felt was perfect. I was tasked to begin writing about my feelings and this book is the result of my literary journey. What is stated is the truth of how I felt and perceived the events of my life. My endeavor is not to condemn anyone who was involved. Instead, I seek to help those who find themselves in the position of being angry with God. I even pray that if you are a non-believer, you may find some hope for your situation. Perhaps you, too, can find your way out of an angry disposition.

Are you angry with God? Are you afraid to question Him? Have you and God come to a stalemate? Do you even believe He exists anymore? If you were raised to be a follower of Christ, and not just a church kid, then I'm sure what you feel is in direct conflict with what you know. Even if you weren't raised to believe in God, how often do you find yourself blaming Him anyway?

Perhaps you're angry with someone you felt should have been there for you—should have come through for you but didn't. This can be especially painful when you love that person. Anger is anger and it needs to be resolved. I invite you on my journey of over a decade of struggle, contemplation and realization. It's an honest journey of facing my feelings toward the God that I absolutely love. Perhaps, like me, you can come to a place where you embark upon Forgiving a Perfect God.

Chapter 1

Ouch! That Hurt!

A DEAR GOD LETTER

I feel betrayed by You, but it is impossible to be betrayed by You. You are holy, without sin, and betrayal is sin. Betrayal is wrong and You are never wrong. You're never wrong, right? It's what I've been taught all my life. It's what is in Your holy Word. Your Word is truth; it's the truth. The truth is it is impossible for You to be wrong. Herein lies my conflict. I feel wronged by You.

I am nothing without You. I absolutely love You, but the betrayal I feel makes me push You away. I am nothing without You. Still, I do things that I know will cause distance between us. Yet I just can't leave You altogether, because I'm nothing without You. I am beyond miserable outside of Your presence. This is hell! However, I'm miserable with

You because I'm aware of my selfishness, stubbornness, rebellion and hurt. It's not Your fault. I cause this dilemma daily, but I do it because I can't face the truths of what I feel about You and what You allowed. I hide behind things and use them to escape real conversations with You, because I cannot comprehend this side of You.

I can't believe someone, Someone like You, whom I love so very much could hurt me like this. It reminds me of when I scraped my skin after falling. The scrape hurt, but when my parents sprayed that solution on it to disinfect and heal it, the sting was worse than the actual injury. It might actually be the first time I felt resentment toward my own parents. I understood being punished for doing something wrong but falling wasn't done on purpose. It was an accident. It wasn't my fault. My mom and dad were supposed to bring me comfort when I hurt, but instead more pain was inflicted by their hands. They said that it would help the scrape feel better, but instead it just made it sting more. So, I made them aware of how I felt by saying, "Ouch! That hurt!" Of course, they offered words of comfort, blew on it and gave it a kiss; but I found that I was still dwelling on the pain. It didn't matter that the scrape did heal. All I could really remember was the pain. It then became difficult to trust them the next time I got hurt. As soon as I saw the bottle of that horrible spray, I recoiled and begged them not to use it. They told me the same thing they said before, that it would help, but all I could remember was the pain. How can I continue to trust them? Children are supposed to be able to trust their parents. So, I just trusted them. Then it stung, again. The pain was still just as intense as before. I decided that the next time I was not going to allow the pain to happen again no matter how bad I injured myself. That spray was not coming anywhere near me. That's when they did a horrible thing. They held me down, sprayed it anyway and made me suffer against my will.

Parents, however, are human. Humans are frail. Humans make mistakes. Humans design imperfect solutions to problems. Humans mean well, but still cause each other pain. At times they do it on purpose and other times hurt is not the intention. It just can't be helped because they're human. You, however, are not human. You are not frail. You don't make mistakes. Your solutions are flawless. When You mean well, it is well. Your intentions are not just pure, they are perfect. You do not have the excuse of being human. You don't have sin as a defense. When You cause pain, it cannot be justified by miscalculations and uncertainty. You are omnipresent, omniscient, omnipotent. So, when You cause pain, it is on purpose and for a purpose. Even when You're not the cause, You still allow it to happen and it is still on purpose.

Don't get me wrong. I know I deserve pain for many of my actions. I know I need pain to help me learn lessons. I know I must endure pain because life is full of it. To be honest, I feel I've been pretty understanding and even cooperative when it comes to this side of You. In times past I've always turned to You in times of pain no matter the reason for it. You've always been such a comfort even when I deserved to hurt. I've always felt Your love and forgiveness, felt Your understanding, felt Your hugs and concern. You've never failed to be there for me when I hurt. I know You are still there for me now, it's just this time it hurts too much. It's like instead of one or two quick sprays, You turned the whole bottle upside down and just poured its contents on my wound. Then as if that wasn't enough, You rubbed it in — hard. You weren't gentle at all; at least not that I could tell. You heard my very loud cry. "Ouch! That hurt!" Now You offer those words of comfort, but I don't even want to hear them. I know that others in the world suffer a great deal more than I ever will. I recognize this fact. However, I really don't have a true point of reference and can only go by what it feels like to me. The pain is too much for me. I'm not them. Yes, I'm bearing it, but not very well. I don't want to hear what You have to say, though if You stopped talking to me, I would be devastated. All I can do is keep repeating the same mantra over and over again.

Ouch! That hurt!
Ouch! That hurt!
Ouch! That hurt!

The longer I repeat the phrase, the less satisfied I am at telling You that it hurts. I've now started to color the phrase with profanity. The good little Christian girl who dedicated her entire life to You and Your people wants to cuss You out. It hurts to admit that, but You've never been afraid of my honesty; I'm not about to start lying to You now. I'm so angry with You. I'm so disappointed in You. I'm so disgusted by what You have allowed.

I know that others have gone through my same trauma and seem to have handled it well. Most of the trauma I've gone through, I've endured well. It's just this one tragedy. The one thing I didn't think You would allow for my life. I really think I would have taken everything else but this. Then again, who am I? I don't know the future like You do. I don't even know me like You do. It's just that I don't understand how You can give me a passion for something and then snatch it away as if it just didn't matter to me at all. What is more astonishing is that having this one passion stripped from me caused me to lose passion for everything else. I was a faithful, dedicated woman. I was a forgiving woman. I was a loving woman. I was a woman full of joy and life that laughed and shared a brilliant smile with others. I was fun to be around. I had a passion for children and music. I had a passion for Your Word. I had a passion for souls. I was dedicated to doing what was right for the sake of doing the right thing.

I tried to prepare myself for one marriage. I made up my mind as a child that divorce was not an option. I studied how to be a good wife. I studied how successful relationships worked. I listened to the wisdom of Proverbs and the elders you placed in my life. I saved myself. I know I didn't do it perfectly, but for the most part I maintained my decision to marry truthfully in white. I was a 34-year-old virgin and would have remained that way if You told me that's what You wanted. I even told You I would rather remain single than to fail at marriage. Do You remember that conversation? Of course, You do. It was right before he approached me and asked if we could exchange information.

During the whole courtship I constantly reminded You that if this wasn't it, please tell me and I would comply. It's not like I hadn't cut off previous relationships. You just continued to assure me that this was Your will through direct words from You in prayer and confirmation from other people and events. You made it so plain to me because You knew if I wasn't 100% sure, I wouldn't go through with it. I proved to You over and over that if it wasn't You, it wasn't going to be. Even four days before the wedding I was willing to call the whole thing off if it wasn't Your will. What did You do? You sent yet another sign for me to move forward. I ask myself repeatedly if I misunderstood Your instructions. I wish that were the case. Then I could simply blame it on my error in judgment, ask for Your forgiveness and move forward with my life. Even if no one else believes me, we both know that I heard You correctly and my marriage was ordained by You.

I hate divorce and I hate lies. I distinctly recall informing him that divorce would never be my option and that if it was an option for him, move to the next woman. You are the One who taught me to hate these two things. I drilled this hatred of divorce and lies deep into my soul. How is it then that I have been trapped in — and by — both? Even when I found that I had been lied to for two years and had the biblical reason and the right to divorce I didn't. I couldn't. How could I allow something You ordained to fail? I was too committed. I was too faithful. I was too forgiving. I was ride or die. You knew that about me even if he didn't. I know You did not lie to me, but I still feel deceived. I know it was the human who lied and the human who divorced me, but it was You who ordained the marriage.

I waited longer than most of the females around me because You told me to wait. In fact, You told me to shut up and wait. So, I shut up and waited for You. I waited 34 years for a seven-year marriage. Was that really the best You could do for me? Perhaps that was all I was worth. I know I sound like a disrespectful, spoiled brat. Sorry, this is how I honestly feel, and I just can't shake the feeling. I'm not about to pretend that I'm okay with this. That would be lying. You and I both would know that I'm lying, so I'm not going to bother with the facade. *"Wait on the LORD, And keep His way, And He shall exalt you to inherit the land; When the wicked are cut off, you shall see it"* (Psalm 37:34 NKJV). This marriage was not worth the wait. I can't give another man my virginity. I can't start that over. Even if at this point You give me another marriage that is successful, I will always have the stigma of being a divorcee. Where's the land? All I can see is me being cut off. Am I really the wicked one? Am I, Father? What am I waiting for now?

In my wildest imagination I can't fathom how You could possibly make this up to me. Perhaps You don't feel the need.

Now look at me. I'm no longer faithful. I have unforgiveness and hatred in my heart. I push people away and shut them out of my life. I force myself to laugh; it no longer comes naturally. I chose a career that involved music and children, but I don't even listen to music anymore unless I must for the sake of my job. I still love children, but I no longer seek to be near them. I'm not the same person. I don't like who I have become.

I would have rather been a widow. Why do I say that? Marriage is the act of joining two people to become one flesh, one body. Divorce is the ripping apart of that one body. That act most certainly will result in death; therefore, divorce is death. The only difference is that a widow gets to attend a funeral. She gets to hear how wonderful her spouse was and how everyone loved him. People with good intentions will offer words of comfort whether they actually bring comfort or not. She may even hear how people admire her for being a faithful wife. Then she is allowed to bury the remains six feet under and never see the grotesque, decaying body again. No, I had to be like the boy from that one movie and admit that "I see dead people." I was forced to continue communication with the dead, rotting remains of my marriage. I had to be polite and forgiving because that's what Christians do. I couldn't scrunch my face up in disgust when forced to look at the decomposing flesh of my relationship. I couldn't plug my nose when the stench of death hit my nostrils. I instead held out hope for two years that You would raise the dead. I read about Lazarus, Mary and Martha. I believed in miracles. I denied that You would "bless" me with a failed marriage, but You allowed it to remain dead and denied me access to a gravesite. Even if a widow can't afford a casket, she can at least spread ashes over the ocean. My marriage is dead, and he is still living.

Perhaps I shouldn't say any more about it. I realize that if I continue to vent to You about this, I will reveal how much I wish he were truly dead. Please know how hard this is to admit to You. What true Christian would wish death on someone especially when there is such a good chance that they aren't ready to die? I mean there is more to consider than just a life. A soul that will live eternally must be taken into consideration. I'm afraid, however, that my anger, bitterness and resentment is surely clouding my judgment. I guess since I'm committed to continuing to be honest with You, I'll have to admit that the pain I feel makes me want to see an end to it all. I want to destroy the evidence of the failure and bury or cremate it, so I'll never have to look it in the face or hear the voice of it again. I think divorce is worse than death. Then again even if he was dead, I'm still divorced. I guess at this point it just doesn't matter anymore. It's just more of an assurance that this hurt isn't going to heal anytime soon.

So, I guess You can see why I'm in so much pain. I suppose You already knew. Did You know I can physically feel the effects of this trauma? It's not just an emotional or mental hurt. Silly me, of course You know. You know every tear I shed and keep track of them. You keep them in a bottle and record them in Your book. Your Word does say You are able to understand our weaknesses. This is definitely my weakness. I thought if I wrote this letter, it would help me to sort out my feelings and perhaps help anyone who might read it. I pray You aren't offended by my pain. I hope You can help me work through it.

In Painful Submission,
Your Child

Chapter 2

I Regret Obeying God

Never before have I ever regretted obeying the voice of God. Obeying God has always brought blessings to my life. Obeying God has always kept me out of trouble. Obeying God has always made me look good in front of others even when they didn't understand His commandments for my life. People admired me for my obedience and faithfulness to His Word. Teachers loved having me as a student. Church people would commend me both privately and publicly. Friends turned to me for advice and prayer even as a young girl. Obeying God brought favor to my life.

Don't get me wrong. I had a bit of a rebellious nature. I still do. After all, I was a very strong-willed child and tended to want to have my say in matters. I've had my share of punishments that I absolutely deserved — and probably should have received more. That, however, was generally contained in the privacy of my home. My parents dealt with my rebellion. It was understood that if they dealt with it, then others wouldn't have to correct me. I also understood that on the rare occasions when disobedience crept outside of my home, any responsible adult had the right to administer discipline and that I would receive further discipline once my parents found out. Disobedience just wasn't worth it to me. So, I tended to be a good girl in public. One friend of mine told me that members of my former denomination referred to me as "the sweetheart of the state". To me gaining that nickname was a direct result of obeying the voice of the Lord.

I'm not saying that obeying God was always easy. Obeying was definitely not always the easiest route to take. Many of the rules and regulations I adhered to left me outside of popular circles. There were even times when it caused me not to be in any circle except the one of total isolation. Time and time again I was made fun of and called unfair names just because I followed rules. Family and friends would try to get me to sneak and do things, but for some reason I just didn't want to be disobedient to my parents or to God. Not only did my parents have direct communication with God and would probably find out anyway, but I had my own relationship with Him, too. I became a Christian at a young age and had developed a very deep love for the Lord. I held fast to the Scripture that said, *"If you love me, keep my commandments"* (John 14:15 NKJV). That love helped me to make some tough decisions when it came to choosing to do the right thing.

I only had regrets when I didn't make the right decision to be obedient. All those small instances when I was led by God to do something but allowed fear to hinder me left a sour taste in my mouth. There were so many times I would see the result of my not following the voice of God. This would cause me to wallow in self-pity over my lack of obedience. My entire life proved that I was better off listening to God and doing exactly what He instructed me to do.

Obeying God has kept me safe. I shied away from situations in which others found themselves. I truly believe that if I did not avoid those situations, I would have been caught up in a world of drug and alcohol abuse or become a gambler or promiscuous. To this day I've never touched cigarettes, alcohol or drugs. People are so surprised when I tell them that. I've often been asked whether I regret not doing many of the things other young people my age tried. The answer is, "No." I've been spared so much that I really couldn't possibly regret following orders. Were there times when I wasn't safe in my life even though I was obedient? Well, yes, there have been. I was sexually molested as a child. However, that was due to someone else's disobedience. Even in those instances my virginity could have been easily taken, but God spared me of that experience. Obeying God has always been the right decision for my life.

Have I been tempted to do those things? Yes, more so now than ever. Depression has a way of making you want to rebel against everything you know. It has a way of pushing you toward giving up on life and love no matter how good your life truly is and how much you are truly loved. Remember what I said before about what Jesus said? You show Him love through your obedience. Just as I interpret words of affirmation as love, He interprets acts of obedience as the same. I've always had a deep love for Him, so deep down I want to obey. How could I ever regret showing someone I truly love that I love Him? To be honest, I've never had a reason to regret showing Him love in the past. God has been so good to me, so loving to me. I've been overwhelmed with the love He's shown to me. Have I been tempted? Yes, but love kept me away from those temptations and I've never regretted it.

Have there ever been things in my life that communicated the opposite of love? Yes, more so now than ever. If you have to ask, you must think I'm some sort of life form other than human. Of course, I've done things that were the total opposite of His instructions. I may not have ever partaken in certain sins or allowed certain vices to overtake my life, but that doesn't mean I've never done things of which I'm ashamed. It doesn't mean I've never dealt with long moments of rebellion. In fact, many of those moments were days, weeks, months and even years. It doesn't mean I've never dealt with crippling addictions. There have been idols in my life that appeared to be more important to me than my love for my Savior. Realize this, though; I regret any and all disobedience in my past, present and future.

In fact, a few years after the divorce I began to live in severe rebellion. My relationship with God had never been more desolate. Some would have even considered me a backslider. Wow, I had to pause right there. Admitting that out loud is more painful than people may realize. I didn't denounce God or anything as crazy as that. I still believed and would never deny that He exists. I wasn't trying to terminate the agreement I made with Him back in 1980. I just stopped doing what I'd been commanded to do every day at that point and time in my life. I had just sort of shut down on Him. When someone who spent most of their life trying their hardest to be obedient and submissive to the will of God finds themselves caught up in the web of defiance it is traumatic and causes great turmoil. My state of mind back then is one of the main reasons I began writing this book. My hope was that at its conclusion I would be able to find my way back into the arms of my Father. Believe me when I say I regret any and every instance of rebellion, but not my obedience to Him.

Never have I ever regretted obeying the voice of God. That is, never...until this. Yes, you're reading the statement correctly. For the first time in my life, I had to admit that I regretted obeying God. I didn't at the time of my obedience. I was excited that He finally brought someone into my life that I could love until death finally came to separate us. I felt that after the long wait, God rewarded my patience, and everyone would witness His faithfulness to me. I was grateful. I was thankful. I was nervous. I wanted to show my appreciation by being the best wife a woman could be, and I didn't want to be found lacking. I was never nervous about whether my marriage would work out. I had absolute faith that God had provided the desire of my heart. All I had to do was dig deep and put in the work and everything would be right. Yes, I expected some rough days. Life is what it is. I expected arguments, but I expected us to work out our issues. I expected compromise because relationships are about give and take. I expected to have to pray through, but I expected answers to my prayers. I didn't expect fairytale love, I expected the choice to love unconditionally.

So, when what I expected didn't happen, I was appalled. There was no way that divorce was part of God's will for my life and if it was it would only be temporary. God would come to my rescue and revive my marriage and we would have a greater testimony of faithfulness and unconditional love. It's the reason why I never truly considered divorce even when I had the biblical right to walk away. When I no longer had to submit to my husband because of his infidelity, I chose to anyway because I truly believed we would work through this issue. I listened to his confession of an old bout of unfaithfulness that occurred two years prior with a calm that could have only been God-given. Even he was shocked by my reaction. I'm normally a very emotional person and can go from zero to ten in seconds. Was I hurt? Of course! I was pained at the thought of my husband having sex with someone other than his wife and then holding his secret for two years. Afterall, I went through those two years as if nothing out of the ordinary happened. Somehow, I knew that we would conquer even this. It was confirmed in my mind when I asked him what he wanted to do with our marriage. When he told me he wanted to work on it and make it stronger, I settled in my mind to forgive and move forward. My forgiveness was a process, but it was solid.

Imagine my shock when over a year later he verbally ripped me apart because he felt I made us late for a dinner engagement. Admittedly, I usually tend to be late. It's probably the artist in me. That time, however, I wasn't. It was merely a discrepancy in interpretation of what was communicated. He said be ready at seven. I was ready at seven. Apparently, I was supposed to assume that meant we had to be there at seven. It seems so minor, doesn't it? Within a month he had moved out of the bedroom...again. Then he was out of the house...again. I stayed in our home with **his** children expecting him to return at any time. The email he sent me about him wanting a divorce barely moved me. He had said things like that before and we always worked it out. Over a year later my pastor showed up at my doorstep with a manilla envelope in her hand. He had given it to one of his children to pass on to me. They were horrified and dreaded giving it to me. They waited a week before they involved our pastor. She took out the papers and read every word of the divorce decree to me because I couldn't even stand to touch them. It still brings tears to my eyes to even write about it several years later.

Where was the forgiveness I had shown him? One would think being late is a much lesser offense than being unfaithful. It was as if he completely forgot that *he* wanted to work on our marriage. He forgot what unconditional love meant. Perhaps he never knew in the first place. Like the woman with the alabaster box, I had poured my love, my virginity, myself out over him. The sacrifice the woman made was worth it because it was accepted by Jesus. His acceptance made the sacrifice worth the amount she spent over His feet. My sacrifice was just thrown away as if it was trash. Love was supposed to be long suffering and kind. It was supposed to believe, bear, hope and endure all things as said in I Corinthians 13. That scripture was part of our wedding ceremony. I endeavored to live that scripture in our marriage, but I guess I was the only one with that conviction.

At first, I wanted nothing to do with the divorce proceedings. I didn't want to be involved in getting a divorce. However, the conditions of the divorce forced me to counter to protect myself; I live in a no-fault state. It was going to happen whether I wanted it to or not and there was nothing I could do to stop it. I can relate to those who must watch a loved one die. I watched my mom as she died of cancer. Watching my marriage die reeked of that same hopelessness you feel; that the situation is out of your hands. There is a fear that grabs you by the throat and laughs in your face as you're being choked to death with overwhelming grief. In the case of my mother, however, I have the comfort of being able to see her again in heaven. The death of my marriage had no such guarantee. In fact, at this point there is a zero percent chance of ever seeing my marriage again. It died and went straight to hell.

In a society where divorce is so prevalent you would think I would get over it after a while. People get married and remarried all the time. For me it wasn't that easy to just let it go. I know couples don't get married expecting to get divorced. However, I have found in my many discussions with others that they at least faced the possibility beforehand. Some even consider it plan B if the marriage doesn't work for them. This was never an option for me. In my mind, despite what society said, my vows were taken seriously. God knew that about me. So herein is my dilemma. This is why for the first time in my life I wish I hadn't obeyed God and married that man. I couldn't see the good in the situation. I now know the story isn't over and I'm not the author of my life. It's just for a time, a long time, I regretted obeying God.

For the first few years after my divorce, I wouldn't even claim the divorce as mine. I wouldn't say, "I'm divorced" or "I got divorced." I would say, "He divorced me." For the first few years I still had faith. My faith in the next year or so dwindled down to hope. My hope slowly but surely turned into regret. For the first time in my life, I regretted doing something I'm absolutely positive God instructed me to do. I've always refused to live a lie and pretend all is just peachy when it isn't. So, I had to face what I was feeling so it could be addressed. This single event caused such a disruption in my spiritual walk with God, it was impossible for me to see or even sense any good about it. I could no longer ignore the doubt that had taken residence in my heart and mind. I refused to deny the regret I felt as if denial would make it go away. Instead, I chose to face it head on and pray that one day, perhaps through writing this book, I would no longer carry the weight of regret.

The process took a very long time. My pastor often reminded me that the position of my state of mind was not permanent. What I was feeling and the heartache I was experiencing was not the end of the story but only a chapter in the book of my life. Often when I read a book, I sometimes look at how many chapters are left to gauge the possible outcomes. It usually works, but when it comes to the book of my life, I have no idea how many chapters are left. I was in a dark place, and everything was negative and felt like the end. I couldn't see how my life could possibly turn out better. At the time I felt that even if I knew how many chapters were left, there was no way God could make this up to me. That was the problem. I started relying on my thoughts and feelings instead of what God had shown me all my life. He was and is still capable of working *everything* that happens together for my good. He works the laughter, the tears, the joy, the suspense, the heartache, the tension, the relief, the resolution... all of it works together by His design using His creativity. He is a master at authoring beautiful, fulfilling, life changing stories.

Jesus was fully aware of this and never forgot what His Father was capable of. Paul brings this to light in Philippians 2:4-11. He writes that we shouldn't focus just on ourselves. We should follow the example of Jesus. If anyone didn't deserve the horrors life brought, it was Jesus. He was God but didn't cling to it. Instead, He chose obedience by giving up divine privileges and humbling Himself, taking on the position of a slave by putting on human flesh and obeying His Father to the point of dying a criminal's death on the cross. He understood that God was not going to allow the story to end there. And His Father came through. Jesus was elevated to a place of the highest honor. His name is above all names. Salvation comes through no other name and the only way to God is through Jesus. There will come a day when every knee, whether found in heaven, earth or under the earth, will bow to His name. They won't just bow; they will also confess that He is Lord. I realize that many denounce His authority, but one day that will come to an end. Even the devil himself will succumb to God's will. This is His reward for being obedient.

Did I regret obeying God for a period of time? I absolutely did. Do I regret it now? No. When I first wrote my thoughts down, I was still in a place of regret. My story, however, continued and I am living in the next chapter. I'm beginning to see the good. I'm beginning to see how He's working the plot of my story. There were others in my story to consider — they needed me to go through what I did and make the sacrifices I made. When I encounter them and watch how God uses my experiences to help them come through, the plot is clearer. When I see hope rekindle in their eyes or a ghost of a smile, the plot is clearer. When I see lives change and people are redirected toward Him, the plot is clearer. The Author and the Finisher of my story is writing an incredible masterpiece. I'm grateful that He is now writing regret out of my life.

Chapter 3

The Impasse

This is ridiculous! All I do is run in circles. The circles in which I keep running are, to say the least, tiring. I'm going around seeing the same scenery, coming to the same conclusions, falling into the same traps. None of my present movements are logical. In fact, in my opinion, my movements are asinine. So why do I continue? Why do I continue to torture my psyche? Why do I continue to repeatedly rehearse the same foolishness? Why do I continue to run around and around resembling the proverbial headless chicken? If I knew the answer, I certainly would not be doing all this running around.

At least running in circles suggests some sort of movement because, well, to be honest I don't run all of the time. Sometimes I just sit there staring at my present position.

I sit and gaze in amazement of how long I can watch myself dissolve into this incredibly intense insanity. My progress is stunted and at times I'm rendered completely immobile. So I just sit. I neither move forward nor regress. I just sit. The more I sit, the more sitting I do. The more I sit, the harder it becomes to move again. Moving around in circles at least feels as if I'm going somewhere even though I know I'm not. Now I sit because I asked myself this question, "If I'm not going anywhere, then why bother moving?" It's as if fear has rendered me completely paralyzed and all I can do is sit and stare at the impasse.

The Impasse. When I first felt that I was at an impasse, I envisioned myself at an intersection in which I was unable to cross. It wasn't an intersection of paved streets. It was at the cross of two dirt roads in the middle of a flat barren desert. I'm not sure why this picture appeared in my mind, but when I researched the word, I realized that my image was wrong. The barrenness was correct, but the image of two intersecting roads was not. The word impasse originates from the French language and means not passing or the opposite of passing. No passage. No way. It refers to a blind alley or a cul de sac. If I were at an intersection, I would be able to move whether it would be a right or left turn or to simply cross the road to the other side. Either way in my first vision I would have the ability to progress. When I researched this definition, it suggested moving in a particular direction but being forced to backtrack or turn around and go back the way in which I came. A church I used to pass often had a certain statement on their marquee: "If you are going in the wrong direction, God allows U-turns." I hated reading that statement. I hate being forced to make a U-turn. It suggests that I missed a turn or didn't follow directions well. Am I really supposed to turn back? There is an undoing of progress in going back the way in which I came. Have I been going in the wrong direction all this time? I thought I was following His directions in the first place. When did I get off track? How far do I have to go back before I'm straight again? Where am I supposed to go now and how in the world am I supposed to get there? Start over? Really? Just... start over? Does anyone besides me realize how long I've been going in this direction? I'm so far gone now that I feel that even if I did turn around the entrance is blocked. My sense of direction is so twisted I can't even go back the way I came to get back to the starting line. I'm sorry, but this is ridiculous!

The Impasse. It's a situation in which it seems no progress is possible. It's a predicament where there is no obvious escape. There is no advancement, no moving forward. This is why I feel trapped. I can faintly see a way out, but the restraints are too tight and there are too many hindrances blocking the way. There are insurmountable difficulties — I'm out of rope and my wings are missing feathers. It is why I feel suffocated. All the pain and disappointment have been stuffed into a pillowcase of anger and Fear has it pressed to my face to complete its assignment of asphyxiation. The fire of failure is issuing out dark clouds of bitterness and resentment that are blocking my airways. It's why I feel as if I'm slowly drowning. I know I have the capability of swimming, but it's too much effort to stay afloat and my life jacket has been shredded by doubt. I'm not treading crystal clear water; I'm fighting quicksand and I'm tired. Why in the world would I continue to keep struggling? Again, this is ridiculous.

The Impasse. It's a dead end. It's an end and it is dead. It has no life. It is snuffing the life out of me. I'm carrying a heavy load and have reached a place of no more progress. The load has become its own dead weight and is crowding and crushing me in this dead place —— this place of death where faith is on life support and my IV of hope is running low. Yes, I understand it's not the end of my life, but it is the end of my dreams and there are no CPR procedures and a DNR has been issued by Someone in higher authority than me. It's a deadlock. I'm locked in the death of who I thought I was, the death of my marriage, the death of my visions and aspirations. How can I trade in my mourning garments if there are still memorials and funerals to attend? "Let the dead bury the dead." That's what Jesus said to do when He asked men to follow Him. The problem is I'm too dead to follow Him in this U-turn. Let the dead bury the dead? Okay, then allow me to bury myself. No? Why? Because I still have a reason to live? Where is it? What is it?

Perhaps my sense of sight is dead because I'm not sure I see the point of living except that I would hate to die this way. Where is the faith I had that saw the invisible? Perhaps my sense of hearing is dead because although I can hear what is being said, I can't make myself listen to reason. That's where my faith is. Faith comes by hearing, but I'm spiritually deaf. Perhaps my sense of taste is dead. I can no longer taste the victory that was promised to me if I were to just hold on and keep pressing my way. I can no longer taste and see that the Lord is good. What is this again? Oh yeah, it's ridiculous.

How did I end up at this impasse? Because of the anger and the feelings of being abandoned I pulled myself away from my lifeline. I have withdrawn from His house and His people. I've never been one to be fake about anything. People are always aware of how I'm feeling by the look on my face or my demeanor. I have an incredible need to be honest and live honestly. That means if I call myself a Christian, I want to live as a Christian. The pain of being abandoned has completely knocked me down. By nature, I've always been a fighter. I had always been a prayer warrior and intercessor. I would fight for people and for their souls in the spirit realm with a fervent holy anger. I hated to see the devil interfere with the lives of God's people and would do everything in God's power to come against the assignments of the enemy. Now I've been hit in a place that knocked the breath of the Holy Spirit out of me. At least that's the way it felt. I've fallen and I don't want to get up. I don't want to fight anymore. I just want to lay here until the referee calls the fight or my corner throws in the towel. But it's never going to happen. The referee is saying I am still able to stay in the ring and my corner refuses to throw in the towel. So, I lay here, and I guess I'll have to take the full count.

When I got hit and stopped fighting the enemy, my flesh got out of hand. I no longer had the strength to bring it back under subjection. I just let it take over. I was in too much pain. My flesh found things that allowed me to escape the overwhelming painful thoughts that ran rampant in my mind. I got caught up and began to live what I saw as a double life. After listening to a message about Jonah and how he had to be thrown overboard because of his disobedience, I decided I couldn't take the pressure of the impasse. God wanted me to accept what He allowed and continue to be the minister He called. I didn't want to accept what He allowed and couldn't continue to live a double life. I had gotten caught up and I knew it was up to Him to deliver me. I couldn't understand why He hadn't brought the permanent change I so desperately needed. I absolutely refused to pretend that all was well. I couldn't. How could I preach and teach about living holy when I was so caught up myself? I found myself even more trapped in this impossible situation. So, I jumped overboard so my pastor, the captain of the ship, wouldn't have to throw me over. God and I were truly at an impasse.

The Impasse. It's the place where two sides that are negotiating are unable to compromise and come to an agreement. An impasse such as this is harmful for both sides whether directly or indirectly. One or both sides may choose to take direct action against the other to force compliance to their way of thinking. In a more indirect manner neither side budges and nothing is accomplished. The impasse makes it clear that each side's position is genuine and not just an ambit claim. In other words, neither side is making outrageous demands just to get the other side to counter-offer in their favor. Both sides see and interpret facts their way and it becomes difficult to see the other side as being reasonable or fair. This is when it may be advantageous for both parties to seek a mediator.

A mediator is a third party that occupies a middle position and attempts to help two sides who are in conflict come to a resolution in a dispute. Judges would just rule one way or the other as they see how the law is to be interpreted. The mediator is there to increase communication, minimize harm and maximize agreement. They are an intervening agency that indirectly exhibits causation, connection and relation. A mediator facilitates the prevention of interference to the process of coming to a mutual agreement. Mediators go between, referee and stand as middlemen in order to settle differences. Mediators are preferred due to the opportunity of both parties having a say in the outcome of negotiations and giving both sides more of a feeling of control. Both parties are more willing to comply because they were directly involved in the resolution.

Having disputes brought before the court means the conflict becomes public record. Mediators have strict codes of confidentiality and as I understand it many will destroy any notes once a resolution has been found. Mediators are considered more cost effective because they tend to keep disputes out of the court systems where months of court costs can multiply daily for years. Entities of mediation often have ideas and points of view that may not be obvious to those who are in conflict. Their ideas often bring calm and a fresh perspective to a volatile situation.

God and I are at an impasse. I have walked into an immovable holy wall of "no" and can no longer go the way I've been going. He says I must do things His way. I say His way isn't fair. He says I must turn around. I say I was following His directions in the first place. Why am I now made to feel I've been going in the wrong direction? He says that His decision is best for my life. I say His decision is destroying my life. He says as my Father He knows what is best for me. I ask how my Father could bring me so much pain. He reminds me of His Son.

His Son, Jesus, the Mediator. "For there is only one God and one Mediator who can reconcile God and humanity— the man Christ Jesus." (1Timothy 2:5 NLT). It appears that God knew all along, before time began, that He and I would meet at this standstill. I imagine that He's been here waiting for me to arrive. Not only did I need Christ to be a mediator in order to begin a relationship with God, the Father; apparently, I need Jesus to mediate now to repair my relationship with God, my Abba. His Word says there is only One. At this point I have no other choice but to listen to what the Mediator has to say. Jesus is here to increase communication, minimize harm and maximize agreement between The Father and His child. Somehow the Son of God must present a way to keep me from sabotaging my destiny. He has always been my Advocate, pleading my case when I found myself deep in sin. Now can Jesus find a way to get past my stubbornness and rebellion and help me be willing to comply with our established agreement?

Can this Mediator convince me that He is truly the middleman? I know He is God and can plainly see God's point of view, but does He understand mine? I know He is in total and complete agreement with the Father, so how can He be a fair go between unless He understands how I feel? Can I trust Him to cover me in my stupidity or will He expose me for my treacherous behavior? I'm aware that He paid the ultimate price at Calvary, but what is this going to cost me? Has He ever been at an impasse with the Father? Has He ever come to a place in His life where He did not want to do it God's way? Has He ever struggled with what God the Father was allowing to happen in His life? Ah, yes...Gethsemane. This was definitely a place of impasse.

Gethsemane was a garden that Jesus prayed in right before He was arrested. The name means oil press. He was certainly in a press to do the will of His Father. He understood what God wanted from Him and it made Him extremely sorrowful and heavy. In fact, He was in sheer agony over what He had to face. When you read the accounts of His prayer in the Gospels, you get the feeling that Jesus really didn't want to go through with the plan.

He was facing an agonizing punishment and an even more agonizing death. Even beyond the torture and death, He had to take on the sin of the entire world. He had to take the punishment for every person that ever lived, was currently living and who would live in the future. He had to face His own Father forsaking and abandoning Him in our place. As the time approached for this to take place the Son of Man just really wasn't feeling it. Yet, it was what God demanded. I can completely relate to how Jesus must have felt. He didn't sin. We did. This punishment was for us, not Him. This wasn't His fault; the fault was in humanity.

I find it interesting that each of the Gospels recount the prayer Jesus prayed in a slightly different way. Allow me to highlight portions of each prayer. In Matthew's account (NKJV), Jesus uses the phrase,

"If it is possible, let this cup pass." In Mark's account (NIV), the phrase is "Everything is possible...take this cup." In Luke's account (NIV) He prays "If You are willing...take this cup." The differences between the accounts may seem slight, but it shows the different emotional states through which Jesus must have gone. The Bible says in Matthew and Mark that Jesus prayed three different times in the garden. The number of times He returned to the garden is not as clear in Luke's account, but it does show that He continued to pray about the same situation.

In Matthew Jesus prayed, "If it be possible, let this cup pass." Since Jesus is God, why would He pray as if He wasn't sure whether God could come up with another way? Why did He use the word "if"? It seems that He was simply declaring that there is a possibility of being able to take another avenue. Another way to look at it is He was making a request to the Father. It's obvious His flesh was talking. It seems that He had a thought to find another way to do things. In other words, He seemed to be pondering the possibility. There is a sense of questioning what is happening and if what is happening is necessary. What emotion is He demonstrating? Could it be that Jesus was suffering consternation? Did He experience a sudden disappointment that caused Him confusion, dismay or distress? The Bible does say He was in great agony. It feels like a child asking a parent, "Aww, do I have to do it?" He, however, made it clear that He was willing to do as He was asked. It seemed that by the time He concluded His prayer, He relented. The distress He felt caused Him to make a request, but as He continued in prayer He eventually yielded to the will of God. He requested and then He relented.

In Mark Jesus prayed, "All things are possible, take this cup." This sounded like a demand. It's as if through prayer Jesus solidified His knowledge that His Father had the ability to find another way. He knew God could do this differently, but instead the Father wants to stick with the original plan; the agonizing, painful plan. Here I sense frustration and perhaps anger. The Bible is clear that Jesus felt both emotions at other times during His ministry. I don't believe it is a far stretch to imagine Him feeling the same as He agonized over His coming death. He yet again had to deal with the speech of His flesh. Now the child is saying, "Aww, I don't want to do it!" The frustration and anger at His situation pushed Him to demand another way, but He still ends this prayer deferring to God's will. He demanded and then He deferred.

In Luke Jesus prayed, "If You are willing, remove the cup." When I read this, I can feel the desperation pouring out. He was solid that this is what God wants even though He knew His Father could change the requirements. He couldn't very well demand a change in plans because God is in control. Now it seems He is begging His Father to let Him off the hook. He no longer questions God's ability, but simply begs Him to change His mind. I'm not saying that Jesus was whining, but there is a flavor of could I possibly change Daddy's mind. The child is now pleading, "Please don't make me do this." The despair drove Him to beg for a change of heart, but by the end of the prayer Jesus bowed His will to the will of the Father. He begged and then He bowed.

Whatever emotions Jesus went through in the garden, two things have become clear to me: He understands what it is to be at an impasse with the Father and He is no longer stuck in that place. Somehow this revelation encourages me to look to Him to be the Mediator between myself and the Father. He knows how I feel because He experienced it and He was successful in finding a resolution. After all, He currently enjoys a beautiful relationship with the Father as He is seated on the right hand of God. He fulfilled His purpose and destiny, and He still advocates for those who are part of the body of Christ. So, what is it that Jesus did that brought Him guidance through the impasse experience? How did He go from requesting to relenting? What changed His demands to deference? How did He forego the position of begging to His position of bowing? The one thing I can see in the Scriptures is that He prayed.

Not that I have anything against friendships and relationships here on Earth; but when Jesus was at His impasse, His friends couldn't help Him. It's not that they didn't want to help, they just didn't have what Jesus needed. Peter was willing to fight and cut off ears, but that's not what Jesus needed. He needed prayer. He asked His friends to pray with Him, but they were exhausted and kept falling asleep. So, Jesus found Himself alone in prayer. It was only through prayer that Jesus came to a place of relenting, deferring and bowing. It was prayer that caused Heaven to send angelic help and give Him strength. It was through prayer that Jesus arrived at a nevertheless attitude. He said, "nevertheless, not what I will, but what You will" (Mark 14:36b NKJV).

I look at nevertheless and see three words: never, the, and less. If I switch them around, I see the never less. He developed the never less than what God wants attitude. It was never anything less than God's will for Him. Even though Jesus was not feeling the plan, He followed it. Despite the agony the near future held for Him, He endured it. Jesus never chose anything less than full surrender. He trusted the Father to not just see His side of things, but to see the best side of things. Even before He came to the garden, He settled His surrender in His spirit. In John 12:27, He expressed that His soul was disturbed. He then asked the disciples whether He should ask God to save Him from what was to come. He answered the question by telling them that this is why He came in the first place. Despite this determination He still had an impasse experience. Still through prayer, Jesus found the faith to believe that the pain endured was absolutely needed to fulfill His purpose. Jesus did it God's way and got the very best results possible. In fact, the results were perfect because they flowed from a perfect God.

Jesus had to go through this prayer process more than once. When I first got divorced, I prayed. I was determined to go through this test like a champ. Like Peter, my spirit was willing to go the distance. Unfortunately, I followed the latter example he and the other disciples displayed. The effort it took to be forgiving left me fatigued. Expending energy to love unconditionally left me exhausted. Trying to move forward left me tired. My flesh was weak, and I fell asleep. Yes, I was awakened and prompted to continue to pray, but the effort to persevere caused my eyes to droop and my head to nod. I didn't realize how much I needed Heaven's help until it was too late. By that time, I didn't even want to be near the Father let alone talk to Him. Jesus was rewarded with angelic aid as He continued to go to the Father in prayer. Since He was the only one in the garden who continued to pray, He was the only one who had this experience. The disciples' lack of prayer that night led them to experience separation from each other and the inability to remain loyal.

The Mediator's fresh perspective is that I must increase communication with my Father. My unwillingness to continue communication in the past has thrown me deeper into the impasse. I'll never be able to find my way out or even gain a desire to come out if I don't restart my prayer life. It's not that I stopped talking to God, but the conversation between He and I changed. Arguing replaced communion. Blame replaced worship. I found myself repeatedly rehearsing my hurt. Jesus prayed until the angels came down and strengthened Him. He was in a world of hurt and agony, but He didn't allow the hurt to overwhelm His mission. Increased communication will eventually minimize the hurt. We as humans find it difficult to forgive when the hurt still hurts. It's when the hurt is minimized that agreement can be maximized.

So now perhaps the impasse feels like such a dead end because my prayer life is dead. My situation seems impossible because I didn't persevere in prayer until help arrived. Did I get discouraged because it didn't seem that my prayers were successful? Did I forget about Daniel who prayed but didn't get an immediate answer as he was used to receiving? I suppose it slipped my mind that Gabriel explained to him that the prince of the kingdom of Persia held him up and Michael had to come and help. Perhaps I don't pray with enough intensity. Jesus prayed until sweat like great drops of blood poured to the ground. Whatever the case may be, it is clear I've shut down. I didn't complete the process. I never got to a place of relenting. As my relationship with the Father began to crumble, I had no desire to defer to His plan. The pain I felt doubled me over causing me to bow, but not in a position of worship and surrender. Now I simply don't want to engage in the type of deep conversation I know I need to engage in with God. To be honest, I'm not looking forward to the corrections He'll have to make within me. Again, how do I escape the impasse with a dead prayer life? What am I supposed to do now? I asked others to pray for me. I'm sure they did, but could I really be sure they would go to the lengths that I needed? Where is my help?

It has finally dawned on me that He never stopped communicating on my behalf. Paul said in Romans 8:34, "Christ Jesus ... is at the right hand of God and is also interceding for us" (NIV). So, while I was fussing, He was interceding. While I was complaining, He was interceding. While I was whining, He was interceding. I am grateful to the Great Mediator for keeping the lines of communication open between me and God, pleading my case until the hurt becomes manageable and guiding me into agreeing with God and His choices for my life. At this point I feel it will be my only escape out of the impasse.

Chapter 4

It's Not My Life

I happened to be standing next to a friend of mine when his son came into the area. He greeted his son and asked him, "Where's the love?" because he hadn't seen him all day. It was obvious that this was practiced often because the son immediately responded by hugging his father. His father hugged him back and kissed him on top of his head. Then he asked his son how his day went and assured him that he was there for him if he was needed. It was so endearing to me because I've always imagined the father of my children being a loving father like my friend. It brought a smile to my face and made me feel good about their relationship in general. One of my favorite things to witness is a father and his children in a loving relationship.

Unfortunately, as I walked away, I began to sing an old familiar tune in my head entitled, "Why Couldn't I Have That in My Life". I had made it a practice to constantly sing to God—and anyone else who would listen— that this is what I wanted my life to be. Not only was my ex-husband not consistently like this with his own children, I wasn't even able to have any biological children of my own. This old, tired melody always conjured up feelings of resentment and bitterness. A person can only sing that kind of song for so long. At some point it gets old and grates on the nerves. On that day my nerves were extremely fragile, so I became disgusted with my own train of thoughts. I was a person who celebrated other people's successes. Now I had become a jealous crooner whining out the type of songs that really should be forgotten.

It was at that point that it hit me: It's not my life. Having a wonderful husband and biologically birthing beautiful children is not my life. What I dreamt my life would be is not my life now. No amount of temper tantrums or crying was going to change that fact. At my age, I will not be having my own children. Although I had a great father, I was not married to one. In fact, I'm not even married anymore. It's not my life. Even if I marry someone else and have a wonderful marriage, I will not have the testimony of being married to only one man. It's not my life. I can cry over the spilled milk, but the milk will never be good enough to put back in the glass to drink. I consider myself somewhat intelligent, but it's taken me a very long time to realize and accept that my hope is never going to match my reality. There is nothing to gain by remaining in a resentful, bitter and regretful place. I must realize that if I don't find a way to accept that what I wanted in life is not going to be my life, I will end up in a suicidal state of mind. I may not actually commit physical suicide, but I'm on the road to committing spiritual and emotional suicide. I'm slowly killing my spiritual walk with God and my emotional sanity, because I'm not facing and accepting the truth. I've got to find the path to being okay with what my life is. I've got to get to the point where I accept that what I wanted is not what I have. It's not my life.

I have begun to ask myself some questions. Is this part of the cure? Is this at least one of the keys to forgiving a God who is perfect? If it is, how do I get to the place where I accept what God has allowed? How do I accept the life He has designed for me instead of holding this unwanted life against Him?

These questions have led me to look up the word "accept". This word seemed to jump out at me and began to make a large imprint in my brain. Several of the definitions came very close to making me angry. All of them were successful at keeping me frustrated. Each definition began to speak to me or rather the Lord began to speak through each definition. Come go on this journey with me. Perhaps at the end we can both accept what God has allowed into our lives.

The first definition is to take or receive something with approval or favor. Accepting what God has allowed means I'm supposed to take or receive this life that I don't want. Not only am I supposed to take it, but I'm also supposed to approve or like it. How in the world am I supposed to like divorce, especially when God said He hated it?

> *"For I hate divorce!" says the LORD, the God of Israel. To divorce your wife is to overwhelm her with cruelty," says the LORD of Heaven's Armies. "So, guard your heart; do not be unfaithful to your wife."*
> *(Malachi 2:16, NLT)*

How am I supposed to like the feelings of failure and loneliness? Am I truly supposed to favor the death of my marriage over its success? This is only the first definition and already the act of accepting what has happened seems insurmountable. Liking what God hates seems like an oxymoron to me. Approving something that overwhelms me with cruelty doesn't even make sense. No wonder I get angry and frustrated when I'm told to accept what God has allowed.

The second definition I read is *to agree, consent or accede to something*. It's what happens when someone accepts a treaty or an apology. This speaks more of surrendering. It's the definition used when one gives in to someone else's wishes. It speaks of yielding or giving permission. In this case I'm asked to give God permission to allow divorce in my life. I'm asked to surrender to what has occurred and give it the right of way. It's just that it still leaves me with the question, "Why would God ask me to surrender to something He hates?" Perhaps it's just that He wants me to give Him permission to do whatever seems good to Him. This is when my anger arises. Why would and how could divorce be good for my life? Wouldn't it have been better to never marry in the first place? Perhaps my mind is too small to find anything good that will come from this situation.

The next definition, number three, seemed to be the same as the second one. To accept means *to respond or answer affirmatively to something*. I asked myself didn't answering affirmatively have the same meaning as agreeing. As I continued to read through and research more words, I realized that this definition involved saying yes as if to an invitation. In the second definition a person must accept something that was thrust upon them. It implies force of some kind and one had to decide about an intrusive situation. This third definition speaks of saying yes to an invitation. Are you kidding me? I've been invited to the dance floor of divorce, and I am expected to say yes and go out there and get my groove on. Yeah, right!

The explanation of the second definition spoke of the act of accepting an apology. Just because someone accepted a situation did not necessarily mean the giver of the situation was in the right. The next new definition, the fourth definition, gave me the impression that not only did I need to give permission to God to do what He thought was good, but that I had to declare what He allowed to be true and correct. To accept, according to this definition, is *to regard it as true or sound*. To accept is to believe. It's used as one accepting a claim to be true. In the second definition I could surrender, but still question the validity of God's decision. To question His decision hints at the possibility of God not being right. In the third definition I could accept His invitation, but I still don't have to believe it's the right place to go. With this fourth definition, agreeing with God is taken to a whole deeper level. Regarding something as true means you see it that way, conceive it that way, judge it that way. To accept what God allowed in my life means that I had to have the same opinion about my divorce that God did. I'm okay with His feelings of hatred. I find myself lacking in His declaration of divorce being necessary. If divorce was necessary, then the marriage was unnecessary in the first place. Right?

I mean, think about the reasons for why divorce would be necessary. I don't mean frivolous reasons such as boredom or things of that nature. I'm not one to take marriage as just something to do for the moment. It is a vow before God Himself and is not to be taken lightly. Instead think of reasons that put a spouse in serious peril. There is infidelity and physical abuse both of which are dangerous for the innocent spouse just due to the medical harm they can cause. There is addiction and depending on the kind, it can be mentally, emotionally or financially dangerous. In fact, any of those reasons cause any of these types of damage. Having to divorce because of reasons such as these suggest that something was wrong with the marriage. If the marriage was faulty or going to be faulty, why give me instructions to marry this person in the first place? No one can say to me that I heard God wrong. I wish that was the case, but it is not. For me that would be the easy way out. Blame myself. Blaming myself would mean lying to myself. God was extremely clear. I get that God gives both spouses free will, but I also get that God knows what we will choose ahead of time. What this leaves me with is accepting that God ordained a faulty marriage that was not good for me and then used something He hates to set me free. Then I must see, conceive and judge this action to be true and correct. Is there anyone else out there that feels my struggle with this?

The fifth definition I'm going to address is *to receive or contain*. The example given was of an electrical socket accepting a particular kind of plug. I was going to overlook this definition thinking it really didn't apply to this topic but then a thought occurred to me. *For the socket to accept many types of plugs it must be designed a certain way.* Many times, when something is forced into something that doesn't fit, it could become detrimental to the user. I imagined myself trying to plug a three-pronged plug into a two-hole socket. It not only looks weird, but the electricity would not be able to flow properly. Not only would it not work properly, but it could also cause damage to the plug or a shortage or fire. Things have a design for a reason. It reminds me of a song I used to sing often. The song was a prayer to God to "mold and make me". It's apparent that something must change in my current design before I can really accept what has happened in a way that it safely fits. If I continue this path of being a misfit, I'll eventually do more than just look funny. My spiritual electricity is already not flowing well and I'm in danger of short-circuiting my life and setting it on fire. There is a purpose for me going through this, but that purpose could end up with a damaged prong. I could end up not fulfilling the destiny for which God has designed me. I realize at some point I must allow God to answer the prayer of that song and be redesigned. I need a serious makeover.

Along these same lines comes the sixth definition. To accept is *to regard something as normal, suitable or usual.* This definition caused me to realize how abnormal the will of God has been to me lately. There was a time when I felt the safest when I was in His will. This sense of safety has been missing for quite some time. I'm not my usual self and cannot fathom this situation as suitable. This new life has pushed me to do some very unusual things. I've cut myself off from my spiritual family. I've been hiding in a cave of addiction away from God as if I could hide from Him in the first place. Nothing I currently experience is normal for me as a Christian. Again, this life doesn't seem to fit.

It's not normal for me to avoid the House of God. It's not suitable for me to stop praying. It's unusual for me to shun His Word. I realize that what I've done is pushing me into a life unsuitable for a child of God and it doesn't fit.

If you're thinking there aren't any more definitions for this one word, think again. I'm not even addressing every definition and I still have a few more to work through. The next definition is *to understand*. A dear pastor friend of mine once said in one of his sermons that to "understand" meant to "stand under" the same point of view. I believe it goes along with sharing God's opinion. As I remember, my friend's point was that we move to stand under God's viewpoint. The more I look at the concept of accepting what God allowed, the more I realize that this will take more than a natural effort. It's becoming extremely clear that faith must be the vehicle through which acceptance will arrive. Unfortunately, this leaves me in a quandary. After all, it is what God has allowed that seems to have damaged my faith. How do I have faith to stand under something that damaged my faith in the first place? It puts in my mind this image of me being caught in an avalanche of boulders. The violent rockslide crushes my legs, immobilizing me. I use all my strength to free my legs from the rubble and pull myself to a place of shelter. Then after escaping the rocks, I'm asked to move back under the rest of the avalanche. All I really have strength to do is scream out in pain and frustration, but I'm being asked to move through this pain and stand under what God has allowed.

When a person accepts the office of president, he *undertakes the responsibility, duties, honors, frustrations, decision making and all else that comes with the work of the position*. I'm sure it's painfully obvious that I'm nowhere close to taking on the responsibility of something over which I had no control. What I accepted was the responsibility of marriage. I was prepared to suffer whatever being married brought to me. I was prepared to take on nine children who belonged to other women. I was prepared to submit to a man and trust that God would work out what was not right. I was prepared to wipe the fecal matter from his rear end if he was incapable of taking care of himself. To be honest, I had fallen into the habit of taking a great deal of verbal and mental abuse. I even had one instance of physical abuse. I undertook responsibility for all that abuse by learning that taking responsibility meant putting my foot down to not allow it to happen again. Even at the lowest points of my life, never once did I ask God for divorce. I asked for wisdom. I asked for strength. I asked for tenacity. I asked for understanding. Why in the world am I now being asked to undertake the duty of divorce? Now I have the responsibility to forgive. Now I have the responsibility to revamp my life. Now I have the responsibility to regain my sanity. Now I have the responsibility to deal with decisions that I didn't make without the comfort of the person who made them. Moreover, everyone seems to think I also need to take on the responsibility of letting go. How do you let go of something that sticks to you? Should I take a bath before I get the makeover? And what about the part that does more than just stick to you? What about the part that sinks its teeth into you and won't let you let go? What about the part that grows out of you like a tumor? How do you let go of what is now attached to you? If one more person tells me I just need to let it go, I think I'll just let them go.

The next definition of acceptance is *to receive without adverse reaction*. It refers to a body having the ability to undergo an organ or tissue transplant. The Bible often compares our spirituality to the workings of the body. Even the group of believers is referred to as the Body of Christ. I'm sure this is why this meaning really caught my attention. Great steps are taken to ensure that a donated organ will be compatible with the system of the person to which the organ is being donated. If not, the body will reject what it deems to be foreign and fight against the very thing that has been placed in it in order to save the body. Herein lies my next set of questions. What part of my spiritual body became defected enough that The Great Physician would consider it necessary for a transplant of this nature. Why is my "body" rejecting it with such ferocity? I can't fathom God healing me by giving me a spiritual transplant that appears to be doing greater damage to me. This foreign entity has placed me in critical condition and anyone who knows me can tell I've been placed on life support. I am doing nothing spiritually on my own. If truth be told, I'm barely writing this book. It's funny how writing has become the "plug" to my life support machine, and it is only by God's grace that it fits. At this point I'm going to need some serious spiritual narcotics to battle the adverse reaction that divorce has caused in my life. I need to find a way for my spiritual body to stop rejecting what God has seen fit to place inside of me. It's a good thing His name is Jehovah Rapha, the God that heals. It's the only way I see me ever getting to the place where I accept this life without adverse reaction.

I suppose all of this comes down to the last definition. I must *accommodate or reconcile* myself to my new life. I simply just must accept the situation. It's these two words that tackle me down to the ground. When you accommodate something, you make room for it. I've spent most of my time trying to shut out what I consider a tragedy from my life. I certainly have not tried to make room for it. To me it was an unwanted guest; a tenant that needed an eviction notice. Instead, I'm being asked to give it room in my life, to let it take up residence. Another way to accommodate is to fit in with the wishes or needs of something. In other words, I can't just house this in some tiny hole in the attic. This new life must be able to live in its proper place, and this place must have the right amount of space. Since God has allowed this into my life, this is His wish, or this is what He needs from me. This last statement has probably spoken to me more than any other. If this is what God needs from me, then do I love Him enough to abide by His wishes? Does it matter what the reason is that He needs me to go through this? Not if I love Him. Does it matter how much pain I'm experiencing? Not if I love Him. Is this how I am finally going to reconcile what God has permitted in my life?

Reconcile. Restore friendly relations. Settle the differences. I let this hatred of my new life damage my relationship with God. I allowed a difference of opinion between God and me to manifest itself. I allowed this circumstance to create chaos in this new life because it's not what I wanted for my life. My so-called intelligence analyzed my situation, and I became a judge. God is the only Judge. I belong to Him. He has the right to do whatever He wants with me. No matter how hurt or confused I am, I just simply need to submit to His will and accept His decision.

Deep down I want to be submissive to God. The world has tainted this concept of being a submissive by referring to sexual deviance and degradable experiences. God desires submission from His creation. There are people who seek to be submissive, but they seek to be submissive to people who seek to be gods and masters, and there is only One God. It seems they seek out these types of relationships for completion and may find temporary satisfaction, but unfortunately, they will never truly find what they are longing for in other humans. There is only One who truly deserves a person's act of submission and that One is the Holy One. In His word He commanded wives to submit to their husbands, but He also commanded us to submit to each other. In any case, we do this in an act of submission to our Lord because this is what He desires. God did, however, create mankind to subdue. It is in us to rule and have dominion. I suppose this is where my issue began. Although I tried to be a submissive wife, I ended up rebelling against God's holy judgement. I have flexed my muscles of dominion against His Word instead of against His enemy. Now it's time to just say that what I had planned—what was in my dreams—is not meant to be. I wanted a marriage that would last until death separated us, but that's not my life. I wanted to raise children that came from my womb, but that's not my life. It's *not* my life.

It's not *my* life. This life I call mine belongs to God. In His Word He said, *"For you were bought at a price; therefore glorify God in your body and in your spirit, which are God's"* (1 Corinthians 6:20, NKJV). He also said, *"You were bought at a price; do not become slaves of men"* (1 Corinthians 7:23, NKJV). This is the only way I'm going to be able to make peace with what is now my life. It's not *my* life, it's God's life. He paid for it. It belongs to Him. It's now time to surrender. It's time to give up trying to figure out His plan and allow Him to work His plan in my life. It's His life and His plan and He's going to do this His way. Yes, He gave me free will, but I gave it back to Him when I surrendered my life to His will. It doesn't make sense to try to take it back now. I couldn't do much with this life when I was happy and whole. I certainly won't be able to do much with it as damaged as I've become. So as the old hymn admonishes us to do, moment by moment I'll accept what God has allowed until I've completely accepted that It's Not My Life.

Chapter 5
Can We Start Over?

THE HATRED OF STARTING OVER

I hate starting over! The more time, energy, money or resources I spend, the less I want to start over. It feels like such a waste to me. It causes so much frustration in me. It's a great source of agitation for me. I'll admit starting over is of small consequence when little has been invested and the risks aren't very large. Starting over in this instance can be easily seen as just a learning experience. Better to catch mistakes early when things seem redeemable. However, when I've put so much into something only to have to disregard, dissolve or discard it and start all over, well, um...NO!

I once planted a flower bed in my front yard. I'll be the first to admit my thumb is extremely brown with no green spots of which to speak. (I still love the results of planting, watering and weeding a flower bed.) I really worked hard, spent quite a bit of money, time and labor. I even had pottery and a water feature. All those resources went to waste because flowers hate me. They look at me and just die. Yet, I really loved them, so I started over. I tried it again. I got some help. I spent even more money and tried to do it better. I still ended up not having a flower garden. If I plant it, it will die. I had a guy plant a bush on the side of my house that had purple flowers on it. I got it for $1.00 on clearance. I barely watered the plant. It was still living by the time I left that property. That's probably because I didn't plant it. I had gotten to a point where I felt it was not prudent for me to try again. Every time I walked out and saw my front yard, I felt a tinge of sadness. I hate starting over, especially when I don't get the results I want.

I took a humanities class several years ago. One of our assignments was to make a whistle out of clay. We were given directions on how to shape it and where to place the blow hole. I shaped my whistle according to the directions and it turned out beautiful. It looked exactly like the picture, and I was extremely proud of my accomplishment. That is until I tried to get it to make a sound. Part of the grade was dependent upon whether I could blow the whistle and make a sound. I was sorely disappointed in the fact that as closely as I followed directions, I still didn't get the desired results. We had the option to continue with the process despite the lack of sound, but I'm too studious for partial credit. I had a choice; either I settled for a defective whistle, or I would have to start the entire process over again. There were others in the class that settled, but I was determined to make my whistle viable. Yes, I was frustrated, but there wasn't any other choice for me. I had to start over. I smashed my clay, reread the directions and began again. I read the directions more carefully and I moved my hands slower. It was at that point I decided I would shape that clay until my whistle made a sound. I still have it today and when I blow the whistle, it makes a sound.

When I compare these two experiences, it reiterates my dislike of starting over when I've invested a great deal of myself. The whistle incident happened in one class period. The flower bed disaster lasted for months not including my failures at other residences. Starting over with the whistle turned out to be successful, but now I don't even have that same yard to even start over because I had to give up the house before I lost it. It's no small wonder how I became bitter about my life after the divorce.

It is at this point I need you to realize a few things. I started writing this book in the middle of this process and then I stopped. Right at the time I began this chapter, I was in the process of starting over again. I was trying to claw my way back to God after not attending church for two years. In 2016 I had three major deaths in my family. Then I suffered a few more deaths of people with whom I had very close relationships. Then on the first anniversary of my father's death in 2017, my best friend went home to be with God. Soon after that I went through the process of losing my home and for the first time in over a decade I was forced to rent. The pressure of the grief of more loss flattened me and I shut down again. I was forced to start over in my starting over process. Who in the world needs to start over while they are starting over? My grief was so acute that I was terrified I would lash out and hurt the people I truly loved so dearly, so I spent another two years away from my church family.

THE NECESSITY OF STARTING OVER

I preached a message in 2013 entitled Start Over. It was one of my attempts to make sense of what God was trying to do in my life. Little did I know I would have to turn around and live that message...again. Why do we have to start over? I went back to that message I preached and reviewed the points. There were people in the Bible who had to start over for various reasons. Allow me to share what I discovered.

PAUL

Paul was a devout Jew and extremely zealous for God. He was so committed to what he had interpreted as the right doctrine, he was willing to kill people for its cause. Paul was established in the Jewish synagogue. He had to be important to be given permission to have Christians executed. In the third chapter of Philippians, Paul writes his resume. He talked about how he followed the law, what tribe was his lineage, his position as a Pharisee and how he was blameless in following the Jewish law. However, as zealous as he was, Paul was in complete error. He was ignorant of who God really was and is. He had a form of godliness but was denying the power that was given to God's Son, Jesus. Because of these flaws, God knocked him down to the ground and stopped him cold. Paul was made of good bones, he just needed to be repurposed. God told him his error and gave him new instructions. He started him over with a name change from Saul to Paul. He started him over with a relocation of his allegiance. He started him over with a redefining of his purpose. Paul was given the opportunity to know God in a whole new way but in order to take advantage of that he had to start over. I can't help but to imagine how humiliating this had to be at some points of his life. When he was accosted by God, he was blinded. He had to be led to someone who was a part of the very people he was trying to kill. He had to trust their guidance not only physically because of his temporary blindness, but also spiritually because of his lifelong blindness to who Jesus was. He had to submit to the new authority and deal with their fear of him. He had to be reestablished in God by becoming established in the body of Christ in order to find his place and purpose. He had to prove that he was no longer a threat to the people of the new kingdom. He had to regain his leadership status in order to fulfil his mission of spreading the gospel of Jesus Christ.

I can relate to Paul. I entered my marriage with the absolute devout belief that it would last until one of us died. I never considered divorce as an option even when I had the biblical right to do so. I was knocked down to the ground and blindsided. I was so devastated that I began to struggle with my relationship with God. I eventually lost it enough mentally that I had to take off almost a year from my long-standing career (almost 20 years) in the education system. When I returned to the classroom, I was treated like a first-year teacher. I had to have a mentor who checked on me throughout that first year. I was at a new school and for the first time my location wasn't my choice. It wasn't the choice of the principal either and that was made perfectly clear. I also had a program that was new to me, and the students absolutely loved their previous teacher. It took a while, but I eventually won them over along with my principal. Of all the schools I've taught at, I remained there the longest and now I'm retired from that position. I thank God that He planted other Christians there and all of them have been such a solid support for me in my journey. Still, starting over was horrible. I hated it.

Not soon after this I found myself having to short sell my home. Living in the home of my marriage was eating me alive and I didn't even realize it. What should have taken four months took four years before I realized I needed to fire my agent and get another. The delay caused severe damage to my credit score. I won't go into the details, but I ended up having to rent for the first time since I bought my first home. No one wanted to rent to me despite my previous record of mortgage payments. Once again, I felt I was being punished for doing the right thing and went back into deep depression. I had just lost all the family and friends I mentioned earlier and was suffering with abandonment issues. Still, even in that, God provided someone who knew me so I wouldn't be homeless. Even when I was at my lowest, He didn't abandon me.

I spiritually lost it enough that I took a four-year hiatus from the church. I completely shut down and threw the biggest tantrum a forty-something-year-old woman could throw. During this process I remained very angry with God. I don't normally hold grudges long, but in this case, it was years. I couldn't reconcile what He allowed. I was too blind to see that there was a purpose for what was happening. When I finally came back, I had to reestablish myself. I was welcomed with open arms and sighs of relief, but I still had my personal hang-ups to deal with and it certainly took me longer to regain my sight than it did Paul.

SARAH

In all of this, I think part of my problem was I harbored so much disbelief. Sarah was also guilty of this. God gave her a promise of a son through her husband, Abraham. At first, she waited in expectation, but after years passed with no manifestation of the promise, worry, doubt and fear began to take hold. She decided to step in and help

God out by having her husband sleep with her slave to ensure Abraham had what God promised. God didn't need any help or interference and her attempts to do so led to trouble. After some serious household drama, she and her husband, for a short time, found themselves living in a childless home...again. Later God came back with the same promise He gave the first time. He said Sarah is going to have a baby. This declaration placed her in the position of having to start the process of walking by faith all over again.

She didn't start off so well. She snickered. She snorted. It was a laugh of scorn and derision. It was a laugh of incredulity and unbelief. She didn't believe in herself because she was old. She didn't believe in her husband because he was older than she was. She didn't believe in her God and His ability to come through. This is evident in her attempts to help Him out in the first place. Now years later He's coming at her again with this same promise. Her laugh suggests that she just couldn't understand why He would wait until it was absolutely impossible for her to conceive. She couldn't figure out His "game". Why was He playing with her emotions like this? She snickered. It's what happens when you've been thrown blow after blow, hit after hit. You become cynical, wary, doubtful. You lose your trust in everything. You lose your trust in yourself. How can you trust that God has spoken to you when the outcome of obedience is so devastating? You lose your trust in people. How can you trust the vows people make when you've experienced other people destroying vows they have made in the past, breaking them into billions of pieces? You lose your trust in God. If He allowed something devastating to happen once, who's to say He won't do it again? She had a distinct attitude towards God and His promises. Her reaction to God's promise had to be checked. Her faith had to be reestablished in what God said and His ability to perform.

After she snickered, she lied. I mention this because sometimes this is what happens. If you were brought up learning the Word of God, you don't ever want to appear to be an unbeliever, even when unbelief has settled in your heart. It becomes difficult to face the actions we make that speak of a lack of faith. Sarah is now being given a second chance of living by faith and she is starting to operate in her old way of doing things. In order to start over she had to face what went wrong the first time, so she didn't make the same mistakes. She had to face the fact that she had issues with believing what God promised; Ishmael is proof of that. She needed to be confronted with the truth, so the Lord called her out when she lied. *"No, you did laugh"* (Genesis 18:15 NLT). She did doubt. She did interfere. She did jump the gun. She did try to take control. She was mean. She was jealous. She did complain. The Scripture said she was afraid, so she lied. She allowed fear to ruin the first attempt. God had to call her out on her fear so she could start over with a better chance. He refused to allow her to bring in old attitudes to her start-over. Sarah had to face the fact that she did laugh and what that said about her feelings and attitude toward the situation. Her reaction to

God's revelation had to be checked. She needed to be honest about her need to reestablish her faith in what God said.

It's important not to miss the fact that she had to do something to start over. It was not enough to hear the promise. It was not enough to face her attitude about the promise. The change in her attitude would have to be manifested by the actions she had to take in order to make pregnancy possible. The word of God indicates that she was still a looker. At least Abimelech, King of Gerar (Genesis 20) thought she was beautiful and had every intention of bedding her until God stopped him. What's not clear is whether Abraham and Sarah were still intimate. That didn't matter; she still had to take that step so that she would have the promised son within the time frame God ordered.

I can relate to Sarah. I laughed like Sarah laughed. I doubted like Sarah doubted. I've interfered, jumped the gun, and tried to take control just like Sarah did. I was mean, jealous and a complainer just like Sarah was. And just like Sarah, I had to face the truth. My disbelief manifested itself by my inability to accept God's judgement on how He wanted to use me. Sarah had her own ideas of how God would keep His promise. I had my own ideas of how God was going to keep His promise to me. When my ideas clashed with His plan for my life, I became cynical. People would approach me with all the religious cliches, and I would scoff. At times I became downright angry. I had told God I was His and He could use me anyway He saw fit. When He saw fit to put me in a marriage for the sole purpose of rescuing children, I found that I wasn't fully committed to that declaration. I was committed to give up anything within my marriage, but not give up my marriage. I allowed the loss to overwhelm me, and I didn't want to be used by God. I felt used by God. It felt like He was mocking my dreams and scoffing at my desires, so I scoffed back. He would put people in my life and lead me to minister to them. I scoffed and told Him He must be kidding. But just like Sarah had a baby around a year later, He used me to help people even in my messed-up state of mind and heart. He called me out on my attitude and then still used me.

On a side note, Abraham laughed, too. I had to ask myself and the Holy Spirit what was the difference in Sarah laughing and Abraham laughing. There is a difference because the Lord reacted differently to their laughter. Sarah was called out, but Abraham was just reassured. As I studied this, I concluded that the difference was in their attitude. There was disbelief in them both, but Abraham lacked the scorn Sarah had. It was their attitude that was different. When you truly forgive someone, it comes through in your attitude. If I truly forgive, I can have conversations without cynicism. I can recall the past without bitterness or resentment. I can have a connection without fear and doubt putting a wedge in between and causing further separation. I release the other person from any debt and my right to have an attitude. This means looking at a couple and being happy for them even when I'm single. This means praying for marriages even when my marriage failed. This is not easy to do. I had to decide to ditch my attitude and be receptive to what God wanted to do in my life, through my life and with my life. This included my attitude towards myself once I came into the realization that my attitude was my fault.

PETER

Peter was the first disciple to be called by Jesus. He was one of the three disciples in the inner circle of Jesus. He was the most outspoken and passionate of the disciples. He had a mouth and it was in constant use during his time with Jesus. It was he to whom the Lord revealed that Jesus was the Messiah. He is the only one besides Jesus to ever walk on water. He was prepared to fight and kill for Jesus. He was bold and completely dedicated to Jesus...or so he thought. What Peter had a hard time doing was surrendering. He was willing to die for the cause but when Jesus told him to put away his sword that shook him. He watched the soldiers carry Jesus away and Jesus didn't put up a fight. He began to understand that Jesus wasn't going to go into a physical battle and fight flesh and blood. That threw him. It baffled him so much that he forgot about the conversation during the Passover meal, the conversation in which Jesus told him he would deny his relationship with the Savior three times before the rooster crowed twice. Even though he was warned by Jesus he did exactly that. When it came time to be bold and open his mouth to declare Jesus to be the Messiah, he failed. Instead, he opened his mouth and denied Jesus and cussed folks out. The crowing of a rooster brought him to the realization that although he was first to be called, first to speak up, first to step out on faith, he was first to deny his faith and his friend.

After the resurrection of Jesus, Peter had a face-to-face conversation with Him. Jesus, being who He was, understood that Peter needed to reset and reestablish himself. For every time Peter denied Jesus, Jesus asked about his love for Him. Jesus had not changed His mind about building the church on the shoulders of Peter, but He recognized the need for Peter to rekindle his faith. Peter had to start over. He messed up the relationship he had with his Lord. Jesus simply responded to Peter by relaying the message, "Let's start over." He started with reestablishing the love between them. Peter had been hit hard with fear. Fear of what he'd done. Fear of what Jesus thought of him. Fear of whether he was redeemable. Fear of where he stood now. The Scriptures say that perfect love kicks fear out (1 John 4:18). I believe this is why Jesus started Peter over with love questions. Fear must flee in the face of love. The next part of Peter's start-over was to reestablish his calling. He thought he was called to fight, but Jesus originally called him to follow Him, and He would teach him how to fish for men. He reminded Peter that it was about the souls of men coming into the Kingdom of God by telling him to feed the lambs, to take care of His sheep. He also reminded him that he was to follow Him. This is what Peter didn't do in the garden. He stepped ahead of Jesus and cut the soldier's ear off, then he watched Jesus march off to His death. After Jesus reestablished the love Peter had for Him, He prophesied to him about His death (St. John 21:18). Peter was to follow the Savior's lead and surrender even unto death. Peter had to be put back on the path for which he was destined. Peter could not do what he needed to do and go where he needed to go if he was stuck in his guilt and remorse. When Jesus kept asking about his love, he was hurt at first. Then he made a profound statement: "Lord, You know everything." Jesus did know everything including the fact that Peter loved Him even though he denied Him. Jesus forced Peter to see that what really mattered to Him was love. As long as Peter loved Jesus and Jesus loved Peter, Peter could start over.

I can relate to Peter. I was in church before I was born, developing in my mother's womb. I was taught at a young age about salvation and the love of God and gave my life to God as a child. I dedicated my entire life to Him and His ministry. I always had my big mouth open proclaiming Him to my classmates and peers. I have always been vocal about my relationship with God, and it was impossible to know me for any length of time and not know that I believed in Jesus. I was called to the ministry at a young age and was extremely faithful to my call, so when I finally shut down on my relationship and my calling it really shocked many people. The length of time that I shut down shocked many more, including myself. I didn't think I could have gone that long without worshipping my Lord. I didn't think my passion for Christ would utterly and completely deteriorate like it did. When my rooster crowed, I realized what I had done and just how bad off I was. There were points in my life that I felt I would never return to God. I was too consumed with being angry at Him. I was too consumed with feeling guilty about my anger and my unforgiveness. My pastor asked me a two-part question while trying to counsel me through my overwhelming emotions. She asked if I believed God loved me and did I love God. I was able to answer yes to both questions.

I had a great relationship with my dad. We could argue and say some pretty awful things to each other and then find ourselves laughing minutes later. I think that's because no matter what went down between us, I never doubted his love for me. Because of my relationship with my earthly father, I knew this to be true about my Heavenly Father. No matter what He allowed in my life, I knew without a doubt that He absolutely and completely loved me. As angry as I was with Him, I knew emphatically that I absolutely loved Him. I was angry and hurt, but that never changed my love. When I answered her and told her yes, she said to just start there. It was the only place left for me to start. I had nothing else but those two facts: He loves me, and I love Him.

I now realize that I have some preconceived ideas about God that aren't necessarily true. I made some assumptions about how He operated, and when His actions didn't fit into what I felt should have happened, it shattered my idea of God. I built my beliefs on those assumptions and the finished product came out lopsided and askew. What happens when you build something or put something together without the proper specifications? Usually, you must start over. That's what I need to do. Start over. If I want to get to a place where I can forgive God, I realize that there are a few steps I must follow to get there.

THE PROCESS OF STARTING OVER

CUT YOUR LOSSES

So how in the world do I start over? I think the first thing that needs to be done is to cut losses. Part of the reason I stayed under the oppression of anger for so long is because of what I lost. I couldn't just say easy come, easy go. That's probably because it didn't come easy in the first place. I felt I had sacrificed so much for so little. I wanted to hold on to my marriage with everything in me and the loss crushed me. I had so much of a problem with what I lost, I refused to read the book of Job in the Bible. In fact, for a while I refused to even read the Bible, but even when I picked it back up, Job was still off the list. I didn't want to read about his tragedy because it rubbed against the wounds of my own tragedy. I didn't want to follow his example of how he handled his crisis. However, because the Word was hidden in my heart since my youth, the Holy Spirit brought it back to me regardless and I had to listen. He spoke even when I turned my head and tried to ignore what He was saying. Yet, it was impossible to ignore because it wasn't on the outside of my ear; it was in my heart. Not only did Job give an example of cutting losses, but there are several others who did as well. Each person found themselves in different places that forced them to have to cut losses and each of their stories teach the valuable lesson of how and when to cut what has been lost.

When Job lost everything, including his great wealth and his children, he made an incredible statement, *"...the Lord gave me what I had, and the Lord has taken it away. Praise the name of the Lord"* (Job 1:21 NLT). He cut his losses and continued to praise the Lord. In Job's case he did nothing wrong, the Word of God says that he was blameless. He feared God, stayed away from evil and was a man of integrity. He was an excellent father who constantly covered his children and their possible sin through offering sacrifices to God. There was no reason for Job to suffer the losses that he did except that the devil challenged God concerning him and God accepted the challenge. Even though God maintained strict control over what could be done to Job and when, He still allowed so much to happen. He did nothing to deserve this test except giving his life totally and completely to serving God. Job had no idea why God allowed all the loss, but he somehow sensed that God had a plan and a purpose. After he lost everything, he refrained from blaming God (Job 1:22). Of course, the test didn't end at his loss, and he suffered physically. Eventually he had some things to say. God gave him a verbal lashing that lasted for four chapters. Do you know how Job responded? He said, *"I take back everything I said"* (Job 42:6 NLT). After this, God replenished everything that was taken with twice as much as he had. He even gave him the same number of children that he had before. Here is where I want to point out something. He didn't get back his original children. Material things can be replaced, but people can't. He forever lost his first ten children and—according to the Scriptures—any grandchildren. Nothing was left except a servant that escaped to tell what happened. God gave him ten more children, but He didn't raise the original ten from the dead. Job suffered that loss, yet he didn't become bitter or resentful. He accepted the loss, mourned his children and then moved forward. Realize what he had to do to have ten more children. He had to start over. As he experienced the birth and rearing of each new child, he did it with the knowledge that he had no guarantee the same thing that happened before would not happen again. Job had to totally trust God and that meant cutting away from any bad feelings toward Him for what happened in the past. This man lived long enough to see four generations of his children and grandchildren. He continued to serve God and did not place blame on God. He forgave God. To forgive means to stop being angry, bitter or resentful for an offense. Job is clear about how he felt offended by what

God allowed, but in the end, he took it all back. He cut the power of the loss and accepted the new gift.

King David learned how to cut losses as well. When he sinned against God by getting Bathsheba pregnant and having her husband killed in an attempt to cover his deed, he petitioned God to spare the child's life (2 Samuel 12). Nathan, the prophet, called him out for his sin and declared that the child would die. He fasted and prayed, and God sent the answer to his request. It's just that the answer was no, and the child died. David's people were afraid to even tell him because of how he acted when the child fell sick. After realizing the death of the child had occurred, David stopped fasting and mourning. It was such a difference that he was questioned as to why the change in his attitude. He stated that while the child lived, there was always a chance that God would have mercy. Once God's answer was clear, David acknowledged that he didn't have the power to bring the child back. He stated that one day he would go to his child, but his child could not come to him. David acknowledged that he was wrong for what he did. He lost a moment of his integrity and caused Bathsheba to lose her husband and a child. He could have become bitter and consumed with guilt. Instead, he cut his losses. He didn't just stop there; David started over with Bathsheba. This time the child was conceived in the correct manner. The child grew up to be the next king and the wisest man to ever live. David cut the power of the loss and accepted forgiveness.

Someone else who had to learn to cut his losses was Joseph. When he was a young man, he dreamed of his future. His future showed him ruling over not only his brothers, but his father. This caused an extreme amount of jealousy among his brothers, and they sold him into slavery. Joseph suffered many things because of this. He was stripped of his special coat (a gift from his father), taken from his family, unjustly accused of attempted rape, and thrown into prison. However, what he dreamed came to pass. He was made governor in Egypt because of the gift given to him by God. Because of the way he managed the country's supplies during a famine, many came to Egypt to buy food. Eventually his family also came to him for food. His brothers, and later his own father, bowed before him. Joseph could have sought revenge or harbored animosity toward his brothers for what they did; instead, he cut the losses he suffered and saw the good in what he went through. He lost years with his family but gained more years with them by saving them from starvation. He lost his freedom a few times but gained the opportunity to rule over those who had him bound. Joseph cut his losses and accepted the power and responsibility to save many lives.

Men weren't the only people in the Bible who had to cut their losses. When Abigail married Nabal, I wonder if she realized what she was getting into. I realize she most likely had little control over who she married. Perhaps it was because of this that she became an extremely wise woman. How can I tell? When I read the account of her story in 1

Samuel 25, I noticed a few things. The Bible clearly states he was a fool. His name means "fool" and he certainly acted like one. David and his men showed him kindness by protecting his servants and his flock. Instead of showing hospitality in return, he threw insults to David's men. David immediately gathered his men and was headed to do much damage, not only to Nabal, but his entire family and staff.

What I noticed is that the men who overheard the foolishness of Nabal went to his wife. This says to me that everyone saw Nabal as a fool. It also says to me that this couldn't have been the first time she had to cover for him. They obviously looked up to Abigail who apparently had to fix things her husband was bent on destroying. They told her that she needed to figure out what to do about the mess her husband had created. She had to have had a lot of experience because she moved too quickly and had too much wisdom on what steps to take to placate David. I look at the things she said to David and gather that she was a woman who kept up with current events. She knew of David and his exploits. She also knew David's heart. Considering how women were viewed during this time, this speaks even more of her intelligence and courage in navigating the results of a foolish husband. She had a strong will to live and protect her family and staff. I also believe that experience taught her when to speak to her husband and when to move on his behalf. She did what she had to do and waited for an appropriate time to tell him about her actions. In this case that time wasn't until the next morning.

While she was out bowing before David and pleading for the lives of her people, Nabal was home partying and getting very drunk. He saw what he did toward David as obtaining a victory and wasn't aware of the death sentence David had spoken over his life. Abigail wisely waited until the morning when he was sober to explain what she had to do to save everyone. This revelation caused him to become paralyzed as a result of a stroke—as some translations read. He died ten days later. Now Abigail is facing a great loss. One may think to themselves that it isn't a great loss to lose a fool, but Nabal was the breadwinner. Abigail worked hard to support her husband even in his foolishness until it killed him. It is not clear how long she was married to him, but losing a spouse is hard. I don't know how she felt about his death. Did she have the attitude of 'I'm finally free from that old fool'? Or perhaps she said, 'He was a fool, but he was my fool.' No matter how she felt, she had to face a decision. You see, when David heard about Nabal's death, he sent messengers to Abigail asking for her to be his wife. It's not clear how much time passed, but I can only imagine that Abigail had to decide whether she was going to put herself in that position again. Even if she figured anyone was better than Nabal, she still had to start over. She had to remarry. She had to relearn what pleased and didn't please her husband. She had to reestablish herself in a new household. She was not David's only wife. How did she respond to David's request? She was happy to do it. In fact, she was willing to be just a slave in David's household. Abigail cut her losses and embraced her start-over as David's wife.

Another woman who had to cut her losses due to tragedy was Naomi. When this woman was forced to start over, she reacted much like I did. Perhaps she had a hard time because she had to start over more than once. We can find her start-over story in the book of Ruth. Her first start-over occurred when her husband moved the family from Bethlehem to Moab due to a severe famine. I'm not sure how long they were in Bethlehem, but it was long enough for them to marry and have two sons. The Bible tells us that they settled in Moab and the sons married Moabite women. It seems that the move was good for them as they established themselves in this land. Her first start-over was successful, but then tragedy struck. Elimelech, her husband, died. Ten years later both of her sons also died leaving her with two daughters-in-law. She decided to go back to her home. For a while, her daughters-in-law followed. She encouraged them to go home to their original families. They didn't want to leave her, but Naomi kept insisting. Here is where I really relate to her. In verse 12 of the first chapter, she told them she was too old to marry again and even if she did, she certainly couldn't have any more sons for them to marry. She felt that they were young enough to start over, but not with her. She felt she had nothing else to offer them. Who wants to start over in their old age? I didn't. Especially when I started late in life in the first place. When I look at this story, I see a woman who is sinking down in grief and didn't want her "girls" to witness her low. Orpah finally listened to her and kissed her goodbye, but Ruth refused to abandon her. She was adamant about staying with Naomi. In the seventeenth verse of the first chapter, Ruth declared that God should severely punish her if she allowed anything but death to separate them. Naomi couldn't fight against Ruth's determination. She also couldn't seem to fight the grief. When they arrived at her hometown, everyone was excited to see her, but she did not mirror their enthusiasm. She wanted them to stop calling her Naomi, which means pleasant. She instead wanted to be called Mara, which means bitter.

We see in verse twenty-one that she blamed God. She said she went away full, and the Lord brought her back empty. She said it was Him that caused her to suffer. She had told her daughters-in-law that God had raised His fist against her. I empathize with Naomi. Life can kick you so hard it knocks all the joy out of you, and you become bitter. You forget how loving God truly is. It can feel like you've become His punching bag.

I took some time to research this other name for Naomi, Mara. I find it interesting that it's pronounced maw raw. One of the synonyms of raw is chafed. That's how suffering at that level feels; raw and chafing. Life sometimes has a way of rubbing up against you until you're raw and tender. Events can cause friction that burns and leaves you exposed. When you're in that state, you don't want anything else rubbing against you. Everything that touches you, no matter how gentle, hurts. Everything rubs you the wrong way and in order to protect your wound you may rub back. However, even in the state she was in, God still had her in His hands, not His fist. He blessed her through Ruth.

Ruth still saw value in Naomi. She stuck with Naomi until her mother-in-law got her spark back. Naomi still had life and wisdom in her. She eventually had to cut her losses as painful as they were and move forward. Sometimes the start over is for those who are with you. Ruth followed Naomi's wisdom and brought a fresh start into both of their lives. Naomi cut her losses and became a guide for Ruth.

I think the point has been made clear. People used to tell me to let go. Let go of the past. Let go of the hurt. I would open my hand to let go, but I found that it clung to me. I couldn't just "let go". I literally had to cut it away. Letting go was too passive for me. By the time I was given that advice, the grief had become too oppressive. I had become too attached to the pain and the anger, and I couldn't just "let go" and expect all the residue to just fall away. I couldn't even wash it away as some people advised me. There are some stains of life that won't submit to washing. I had to get to a point where I was willing to cut it away.

Letting go and washing your hands of it are noninvasive maneuvers. Cutting goes deeper and leaves scars. I've had two surgeries on each of my hands. Three of them were endoscopic. This type of surgery is minimally invasive. The doctor used this procedure on carpal tunnel in both wrists and a trigger thumb. Having those three surgeries performed was one of the best decisions of my life. I'm a pianist so losing the use of my hands was devastating. When I came through the surgeries my hands were better and to this day I no longer suffer from carpal tunnel or the trigger thumb. A short time after the surgeries I tore a cartilage in my right wrist. I went back to the same doctor that performed the first three surgeries. This time he was concerned about my wrist and took the time to consult with another doctor before he performed the surgery. I asked him why this surgery was going to be more difficult to perform. He explained the first three surgeries used a technique that only required a small incision into my hands. In fact, you can barely see the tiny scars those three surgeries left behind. The surgery to repair my wrist was going to be invasive and he was going to have to cut into my wrist to try to repair the damage. Even after the surgery, there was no true guarantee that I would have full use of my hand as before. This was so heart-breaking, especially after the success of the first three surgeries. I had absolutely no pain in my hands and could fully use them until the last damage occurred. The tear in my wrist was becoming too much of an issue and I decided to move forward. When I woke from the first surgeries, I was happy and in good spirits. When I woke from the surgery on my wrist, I was hysterical, so much so that they had to call the doctor back in to calm me down. That was an omen.

Physical therapy was long and grueling. I have a two-inch scar on my wrist and some slight nerve damage. I have full use and no pain for the most part, but there are times when I can't feel my middle finger. That is, unless I rub on the scar that's on my wrist, then I have a tingling sensation. Whenever I let go of something in my past, it was like the release that happened during the carpal tunnel surgeries. Opening the tunnel released my nerves and allowed my circulation to flow freely again. Some things are just like that. You just let go and you're free. When it came to the devastation of divorce, I had to have some things cut into and cut off. My recovery time was longer, and I'm still dealing with some odd sensations. However, I'm relatively pain free now and I can once again use my gifts and live my life without too much trouble. What I'm saying is that sometimes things must be cut into, cut away and cut off. Letting go or washing it away won't be enough. When you get to that point you may experience more anxiety and more pain, but eventually you will recover. You'll have a limp like Jacob when he wrestled with God. You'll have a scar or two, but you'll be able to function again. Don't be afraid to cut your losses and start over.

RE-EDUCATE YOURSELF

The need to start over generally indicates a lack of knowledge or a misunderstanding of knowledge. The Lord spent a few chapters re-educating Job on His authority. David had to learn or be reminded that just because he was king, he had no right to play 'god' in the lives of his subjects.

He was reminded that he was not sinless and learned that God's mercy may not look like mercy at all. Joseph had the right knowledge of him ruling over his family, but he learned that leadership on that level comes with a heavy price. Abigail was well-versed in being the wife of a fool, but she had to re-learn how to be a wife of a different kind of man. Sarah had to learn that God's timing was on a whole different level than hers. Paul was probably the most educated of the examples I mentioned earlier. Can you imagine the knowledge he had to relearn? He had to look at all the prophecies in a different light and recognize the same Jesus he was persecuting as the true Messiah.

In my own personal examples, I had to re-read the directions when I made my whistle. Eventually I found someone to show me how to plant flowers and I now currently have a thriving flower bed. I had to relearn some teaching strategies, classroom management and what a good choral sound was. I had to re-educate myself about mental health and how to manage it. The most important part of my start-over is learning how to trust God again. I spent a great deal of time re-evaluating what I was taught, what I thought and how I interpreted the word of God. Re-educating yourself helps to prevent you from making the same mistakes and falling into the same traps. It helps in adjusting your attitude so you can move forward. It also paves the road for you to learn new things. Having to relearn does not suggest stupidity. I often define stupidity as the refusal to learn as opposed to the inability to learn. Undoing old knowledge and making way for new knowledge or learning right knowledge again is more like cultivation. It is gaining or developing a skill or perhaps a quality. Farmers must turn soil over and rotate crops in order to ensure that things continue to grow. There are times when the knowledge we have gained in our lives has to be turned over and adjusted so that new growth can occur. Our ideas, thoughts and procedures all need to be refreshed and we also need fresh ideas, thoughts and procedures. When we stop learning, we stop growing. We stop moving. We stop living.

My pastor once did a Bible study on resetting ourselves. She hit all areas including physically, mentally, emotionally, spiritually and financially. We need to be healthy in all these areas. A reset sometimes means a restart. We cannot live in fear of starting over because it could be a matter of life and death for us. Don't be afraid of re-educating yourself and starting over.

GET HELP

> *If you need wisdom, ask our generous*
> *God, and he will give it to you. He will*
> *not rebuke you for asking.*
> *(James 1:5 NLT)*

The first one you should seek help from is God the Father. The Bible tells us that God not only has the wisdom you need, but He is generously willing to give it to you. He's not stingy with His knowledge. He won't call you out and call you dumb or stupid. Understand that He can help. Understand that He will help. There are several Scriptures that testify of these two truths. When suffering, it is easy to feel that God doesn't want to help. This is when it is important to go back to His Word in order to reestablish the belief that He has the help that is needed. Here are some Scriptures that will help. By no means is this a complete list, it is just a place to start.

1 Chronicles 16:11	He tells us to seek help
Psalm 23	All the ways He helps
Psalm 46:	He is a present help
Psalm 121:1-8	He is an available help
Psalm 147:3; Jeremiah 33:6	He is a healing help
Isaiah 40:29-31; 41:10	He is a strengthening help
Jeremiah 17:14	He is a true help
Habakkuk 3:19	His help stabilizes

God's Son is willing to help. Much of the ministry of Jesus involved helping people. In Matthew 7:7-11, He instructs us to ask and keep on asking Him for help, to seek Him out for help, to knock on His door and He'll answer. When you ask for help, you will get the help you need. He implores us to come to Him (Matthew 11:28). The gospel according to John (14:13-14) confirms that Jesus is available to help you and you need only to ask. All throughout the gospels we find accounts of Him helping people the same way His Father did. He is still helping us by coming before His Father to advocate for us in case we sin (1 John 2:1).

Don't think it is not a family affair. The Holy Spirit, the third part of the Trinity, functions as a help, also. Jesus said in St. John 14:26 (NKJV), *"But the Helper, the Holy Spirit, whom the Father will send in My name, He will teach you all things, and bring to your remembrance all things that I said to you."* Helper is one of His names and the Holy Spirit lives up to His name. 1 John 5:14 tells us we should have confidence when we ask for anything in His will because He hears us. Hebrews 4:16 tells us to be bold when we approach the throne of God in order to obtain two things: mercy and grace. These two things are designed for the purpose of helping us when we need it. Help is here for you from above. All you need to do is ask for it.

Without guidance, a people will fall,
but with many counselors there is
deliverance. (Proverbs 11:14 CSB)

Heaven is not the only source of help available. There are instances in the Bible where help was passed from believer to believer. Before I get into that, let me point out that Jesus Himself received help in His greatest time of need. He had been beaten so badly His flesh was ripped open. He was tasked with carrying His cross to the place of His execution. The Scriptures simply say that the soldiers tasked a man named Simon, who was from northern Africa, to carry His cross for Him. My point is that Jesus allowed this to happen. He accepted the help. So, if Jesus did, shouldn't we?

When Jesus called His disciples, He gave them instructions. He sent them to help people. In Matthew 10:8, He told them to heal the sick, raise the dead, cure diseases and cast out demons. In other words, as you have been helped, go out and help others. In Acts 16:9, we find that Paul had a vision of a man from Macedonia asking for help. How did Paul react? He went there to help people find Christ. Paul also asked the Philippians to help two women who were working with him in sharing the gospel. Proverbs encourages us to seek counsel when needed. Moses was instructed by Jethro, his father-in-law, to delegate the smaller matters to leaders he trusted so that he only had to judge the heavier matters. He told him he would never be able to judge the people alone. If he continued to try, no one would have any peace. There was another time Moses needed help. Amalek decided to attack the children of Israel. Moses sent Joshua to fight while he stood on a hill and held up the staff of God. As long as Moses holding up the staff, the Israelites were victorious. As soon as he became tired and lowered his hands, they started losing. Aaron and Hur had accompanied him to the top of the hill. When they saw that Moses needed help, they found a rock for him to sit on and each one stood on his side and held up his hands until Joshua and the Israelites defeated the Amalekites. I will venture to say that every victory you have in life will always require you receiving help. It's okay to ask for and receive help when needed. Don't be afraid to reach out and get the help you need to move forward and succeed as you start over.

BELIEVE

You can cut your losses, re-educate yourself and get all the help in the world, but if you don't believe, your efforts will be in vain. In the twenty-second verse of Jude, he encouraged us to show mercy to those whose faith is wavering. This means that there are—and will be— believers who waver in their belief. This entire book is my testimony of this occurrence in my own life. Now that my faith is being rebuilt, let me show you mercy by helping to bring you back to a place of belief, also.

One way to build your "believe" muscles is reading and speaking the Word of God. To be honest, when you're deep in the depression of starting over, it can be hard to believe in anything. You feel hopeless, faithless, overwhelmed. You feel like laying down and giving up. Giving up, however, cannot be an option. So, even if it's a small one, just take one step at a time. Believe in one thing and build on that. Let's lift some weights together.

You must believe in God and His love for you. God loved you so much that He sent His Son to die for you (St. John 3:16). His Son loved you enough to die for you (1John 3:16). He loves you enough to call you His child (1John 3:1). Know how much God loves you and know that you can put your trust in His love because God is love (1John 4:16). He tells us in 1Corithians 13:7 that love should never give up, never lose faith, always be hopeful and endure through every circumstance. If He gives us this instruction, then His love must be the perfect example. This is the way He loves us. Believe in His love for you.

You must believe in His purpose for your start-over. Solomon said in Ecclesiastes 3 that He has a time for every purpose, and He will make things beautiful in His own time. If He judges that there should be a start-over in your life, He has a purpose for it. Remember that He has promised to cause all things to work together for your good, if you love God and are called according to His purpose (Romans 8:28). Believe your start-over has a purpose.

You must believe He has a plan for your life that will accomplish that purpose and will end well for you. Jeremiah 29:11 (NLT) says, *"For I know the plans I have for you,"* says the LORD. *"They are plans for good and not for disaster, to give you a future and a hope."* It's hard to believe that anything tragic can be part of a good plan, especially one designed by God Himself, but sometimes horrible things are used by Him to complete His plan for your good.

What we see as horrible and unnecessary are pathways to a hopeful future. Jairus experienced this. He was seeking out Jesus to ask Him to heal his daughter. While he was in conversation with Him, he was told that his daughter was dead. The response Jesus had to this news was to tell him, *"Don't be afraid. Just have faith"* (Mark 5:36, NLT). Believe your start-over is in His plan.

You must believe in yourself and that you're able to go through the process, get through the obstacles and see it through to the end. Jesus was constantly telling His disciples to stop being afraid and have faith in God. He taught them that they only had to have a small amount of faith to move mountains with just a word. We have the example of Abraham believing so much that he brought glory to God and his faith was counted as righteousness (Romans 4:20 and Galatians 3:6). The writer of Hebrews explains that it is faith that is our assurance of what we can't see. The writer also tells us that without faith, it is impossible to please God. Our faith must have action behind it. James 2:14 asks us what good is our faith without actions. Faith will move us to action and action will move us to complete our purpose. Paul said in his letter to the Philippians that he was confident that God will continue His work that He started within His people until that work is finished on the day when Jesus returns (Phil 1:6). Believe that you will finish your start-over.

This is how to start over. Cut your losses, re-educate yourself, get the help you need and believe. The start-over is necessary. It is doable. It is beneficial. It is biblical. Afterall, even God started over.

GOD STARTED OVER

Wait! What? God is perfect. Why and when did He start over? Let's begin with when. Creation? In the book of Genesis, we find the account of God in His role as Creator. After each day of creation, He declared that what He created was good. I agree. There are times I take a moment to look at various parts of nature and I'm amazed at how beautiful it is. I especially love the colors of the leaves of a tree contrasting with the backdrop of a blue sky. I love the sound of birds singing their songs or wind whistling through the trees. I get a sense of calm when I smell certain flowers and don't even get me started when I get a chance to witness a waterfall or rain or snow. I'm sometimes compelled to take the opportunity to praise Him for His handiwork. After creating most of the world, He waited until the last day to create His masterpiece... mankind. Mankind is God's masterpiece as Paul declared in Ephesians 2:10 in the New Living Translation. And He made us for the purpose of worship. That's what Lucifer was supposed to do, but he got fired. I believe he was jealous and resented the fact that God replaced him with us. So, what did he do? He slithered in and tainted God's masterpiece.

He tampered with God's perfection by speaking until Eve began to doubt what God said about what could and couldn't be eaten in the garden. He introduced rebellion into the world. Now the world was full of sin and was no longer perfect. What was good, now was not. Corrections were made by God because of man's fall. He removed them from the garden before any more damage was done. He continued to commune with mankind, but it wasn't the same as it was in the garden. As sin and evil grew God continued to make corrections, but eventually He came to a place of regret. In Genesis chapter six, God declared that He was sorry He ever made man and put them on the earth. He saw them all as evil and corrupt, except one. There was a man that found favor with God named Noah. He had so much favor that God had a conversation with him about His plans to start over. He told him that He was going to wipe out everything except him and his family and a remnant of the animals. He instructed Noah to build a boat and told him that something that never happened before would now happen. It would rain. The first rainfall was catastrophic. It destroyed what God had created according to His will. Then God started over with Noah and his family.

Despite the destruction of the world, man continued to grow more and more evil. God then set out to establish a relationship with a particular nation of people. The nation of Israel became His chosen people and He established laws to govern them. This was only temporary, and He finally had to do His last start-over. This time He provided such a powerful start over that the results that come from it will last for eternity. God sent His Son to establish a new relationship with man. We couldn't redeem ourselves, so He did. When we accept the salvation of Jesus, we become a new creation, the old creation is dead and through Him we get to start over. Jesus became the second Adam (1 Corinthians 15:47). This start over was perfect. Jesus reconciled us to the Father and the enemy no longer has a say over us. Jesus redeemed us back and it's the best start over ever!

Yes, I hate starting over, but I'm so grateful for this one. It is this start-over that gives me the power and the strength to do the same. When I relocated, I decided to plant some more flowers. I received help from a good friend who knew what he was doing. Some of those flowers are still thriving after a few years. Some I've had to replant. What I learned to do is enjoy the process. What I've come to realize is that the result is worth trying again. Every morning I go out and water those flowers. I've watched them grow. I've watched some die. I've watched some come back to life after I thought they wouldn't. I have so much peace enjoying the ones that continue to thrive despite my brown thumb. So, since starting over is necessary and since it's a good thing to do, perhaps it's what I need to do with my relationship with my Father. I was hurt by what He allowed and then I hurt Him because I was hurt. The only thing I need to do at this point is ask Him, "Can We Start Over?"

Chapter 6
Apology Accepted

September of 2018, I finally decided that it was time to at least try to come back to God. I never had a desire to go to any other church but my own. When asked what church I attended, I always responded with my church's name and then explained I was AWOL.

I didn't leave because I was angry with the members or the leadership; I left to protect them from me. At least I thought they needed protection from me. I knew I was in a very bad state of mind, and I didn't want to poison anyone or bleed all over them, especially the children. I was in a position of leadership and had been for most of my life. I had already seen leaders fall while under great pressure and had even experienced the same types of failure. I couldn't stand the thought of someone stumbling because of me. I loved, and still love the people. I found it difficult to decipher what was happening to me, deal with my humiliation and come to some form of understanding about God in front of everyone.

What I thought would be a short time turned out to be four long years. It shocked many people including myself. I spent my entire life going to church, working a ministry and being an integral part of the body of Christ. It was hard to imagine myself doing the opposite. At some point, however, I had gotten used to not being there and after such a long time away, it was very difficult to come back. I tried after two years of absence to come back to one of our smaller campuses where I wasn't known that well, but tragedy struck hard again so I shut down for two more years. I was still just too wounded to stay the course. Then, I was too ashamed that I was too wounded.

I was beginning to realize that my idea of God wasn't His idea of Himself, and my idea of His love wasn't His idea of how He really loved me. That realization seemed to have deflated my anger enough that I was finally willing to hear what God, my Father, had to say about the whole ordeal. The impasse began to dissolve, and I could see that He was just waiting for me to turn back to Him and hear Him out. Funny thing is that this did not start inside the church building. It started during one of my many walks outside. I had started the walks to find my way to health and learned quickly that I'd rather walk outside than on a treadmill at the gym. I would catch glimpses of God's creation and I couldn't help but tell Him how impressed I was. This opened the door for many very small conversations that began to grow until I found that we were communing again. He was giving me small opportunities to worship that I could handle and as I took those opportunities the anger and the hurt began to slowly evaporate. There was finally enough evaporation where I could make the decision again to try to return to His house and the Body of Christ.

The first Sunday I came back to my original campus, I sat in the back of the church with my arms folded and my head down. I spent many Sundays like that. I usually came late and left early and tried not to talk to too many people. Of course, that didn't always work, because my church family was truly glad to see me and they wanted me to know how glad they were that I was coming home. Still, I spent months trying to sit through a service without succumbing to the overwhelming feelings of guilt, shame and despair. It was hard for me because I was a worshiper who couldn't worship. I found that I was irritated during praise and worship. Even though I had those small moments of worship privately, I didn't feel worthy enough to do it publicly. To be honest, I still harbored quite a bit of anger. It felt as if the enemy was sitting on my lap and refusing to allow me to even try to give God worship. What made it worse was that everything was different. I knew none of the songs and most of the people were new to me. I felt alone even though I wasn't. I felt isolated even though I was embraced. I was wracked with guilt for being gone so long. I was used to being a worker, not a bench member. I refused, however, to allow myself to quit again. So even though it took everything in me to get dressed, drive to church and walk through the doors, I was determined to come every Sunday. God had been showing me that once I developed a habit, it would stick. It took four months before I could see any type of change in me. What I started to realize was that God was rebuilding my consistency and eventually it became easier to come each week.

At the beginning of the next year, I finally started coming back to God and not just the church. Things were starting to mend, and I watched the changes He was making in my life. It just so happened that the theme of that year was "Change Your Life" and that's exactly what God was doing. I got involved in activities on a very small scale. It was still a struggle, but I continued to move forward. My Pastor's birthday is the first week of September and this particular year was her sixtieth. She decided to use many of the people she mentored during her years of ministry during the weekend celebration. This included me and I was part of the praise team. She had a conference a few days before specifically geared toward female preachers and asked me to demonstrate a certain style. I hadn't formally preached for over four years, but because of our relationship and her unwillingness to give up on me throughout my ordeal, I couldn't say no.

I used a popular phrase that was going around at that time. It stemmed from what a hotel worker said to a rude customer that was trying to get a room after being racially derogatory toward the worker earlier over the phone. She was trying to convince him of the reasons why he should allow her to stay with the rest of her family. He was trying to convey to her that no matter how desperate her situation was, he couldn't accommodate her because he reported her behavior to his employer. The employer refused to have someone who chose to be demeaning to his employee stay at their hotel. He continued to tell her that the decision was above him and that's the phrase I used for my title. As I prepared this message it became clearer to me how the enemy had been speaking to me over my spiritual phone. He had been causing interference between God and me and I had to remember Who it was that owned me and my service. I had finally concluded that my Employer made a decision for my life, and I could no longer accommodate the anger and hurt that had spoken degradation over my life. I decided to "set my affection on things above" and recognize my deliverance was not within myself. It was above me now.

I stood before the one who had been talking in my ear, reminding me of my pain, rehearsing my anger, suggesting unforgiveness, prodding me to feel offense and faced him head- on. I made a declaration to him and all the demons that had plagued me for eight years. Trust me when I say that they tried to stay in this establishment. They wanted to continue to live in my heart, my thoughts, my desires. They didn't care about all the ugly things they said to me and all the horrible ways they made me feel in the past; they just felt it was their privilege to stay. Afterall, I let them in and entertained what they had to say. Anger begged to stay and tried to convince me he had a right to stay because of all the unfairness I endured. I just shrugged my shoulders and said, "Oh well, it's above me now." Fear and doubt tried to get a room together. They both argued that after being let down so hard by God and others that I should be afraid to trust Him and His plan for my life again. I just shook my head and said, "Oh well, it's above me now." Bitterness had the nerve to ask for a suite. She argued that I should have a bitter taste in my mouth when it comes to relationships. I just stuck my tongue in my cheek and said, "Oh well, it's above me now." God, my Employer, had spoken and told me not to put a question mark where He had put a period. My marriage was necessary; and for the purposes in my life and the lives of those I would influence, my divorce was also necessary. The decision was made above my pay grade, and I simply had to accept it and declare it.

This also meant that the power to follow through with that declaration was also above me. It was obvious that I didn't have the strength to move forward on my own. I couldn't stand up to those demons in my own strength. I had to refer them to my Boss. The authority to conquer all those negative emotions had to be given to me from above. The continual source of that power is above me... far above me. Far above any ruler, authority, power, leader or anything else. Not just in this world but in the world to come. That's straight from what Paul told the Ephesians in chapter one, verses nineteen through twenty-one. Every time the devil and all his buddies try to come back to the establishment I manage, I stand on what the Head Director has instructed, tap into the source of that power and tell them all with absolute assurance, "It's above me now!"

It was during that same weekend that I received something I never thought I would. It was after I finally surrendered to God and made the decision that I was going to do more than just come home; I decided I was going to do His will. It was the Sunday of the celebration, and my pastor had several people speak for her birthday. The church was packed, and the Spirit of God had rested in the room. She invited her nephew, who operated in the prophetic, as one of the speakers. You could tell by the way he got up that something was shifting. He made the statement that as soon as he walked in the doors of the church, he began to receive downloads from God. He said that although he knew he was supposed to give a speech about his aunt, he felt an anointing of prophecy in the room. I assumed that he would give her or the church in general a word from God. You cannot begin to imagine my surprise, no my shock, when he called my name.

Let me first say that I started writing this book several months after my divorce in 2010. There were a few people who knew about the concept, but not many. I took a class twice online to help me focus on finishing and publishing it. I failed both times and in 2016 I stopped writing. I always felt the need to finish the book but just never did. Regardless of whether I finished writing, I was convinced that I would just have to suck it up, move forward and forgive God. He's perfect and not at fault, so the burden was on me to forgive Him. When I heard my name, I thought I was going to receive some type of reprimand for leaving the church or being angry with God for so long or some sort of directive to get busy now that I was back. I began to prepare myself to be publicly scolded. I had been expecting it all year and it was one of the things I was dreading, but I figured I had it coming. I stood up and faced my spiritual spanking like a big girl. The next words that came out of the prophet's mouth totally threw me for a loop.

He said, "God wants to apologize to you." For him to use that terminology left me stunned. I would have expected him to say that God wants me to forgive and let go like I had heard before. When he used those words, I immediately thought of this book. Then he continued by saying that God wanted the relationship that He had with me before my breakdown. He said He wanted my forgiveness for what He allowed so that He and I could move forward in the purpose to which I was called by Him. I had been struggling with forgiving God for years. I always assumed it was on me. Even as he was speaking, I began to question the validity of the prophecy. Then the Holy Spirit brought to my mind a particular Scripture and asked me a question. The question was, "Do you really think I would require anything from you that I don't do Myself?" I received the word that came from the prophet and listened to what else God had to say to me.

So, what was that Scripture? Well, it was Matthew 5:23-24. Jesus was teaching and told the people that if they were presenting a gift to the altar and remembered that someone has something against them, they were to stop presenting the gift, go be reconciled with that person and then come back and finish the offering. I searched the meaning of this word in Strong's Greek. It is the word *diallassó* and it means to change, to change the mind of anyone, to renew friendship with one. It suggests that both sides change in order to renew a relationship. Let me pause right here and strongly declare that God did not do anything wrong and had no need to change. In Malachi 3:6, God declared that He is the Lord, and He does not change. The title of this book makes it clear that I see and understand God to be perfect. Jesus makes it clear with this Greek word that the person offering the gift needed to make things right between him and the one who was offended even if it meant making changes himself. When Job questioned God's decision about what He allowed in his life, he was called out and questioned about his position next to God. When God got through with him, he changed his tune and surrendered to His will. This is what I expected from God, and then some, because unlike Job I was nowhere near any kind of perfection. Yet, there I was standing in the middle of a public service hearing an apology from God. My question changed from "How do I forgive a perfect God?" to "Why in the world would a perfect God apologize to me?"

I'm not even remotely close to being a theologian. I do, however, have a deep respect for the Word of God and having it correctly interpreted. So, after I studied this word, I asked Him what He meant when He brought this Scripture to my mind since there was no need for Him to change for us to be reconciled. He already did the work of reconciliation through His Son, Jesus, and set before us the choice to choose life or death. I knew even in my stubbornness and rebellion that I would have to be the one to choose to change. I'm not trying to make the Scriptures fit into what I want them to say. What I do want to do here is share my testimony and how God handled me and my emotions. I want to share with you what He did for me so that I could be free to do His will for Him.

So why this Scripture and how did He explain Himself to me? The first definition of reconcile is to change. What needed to change first was my heart. The trauma hardened my heart, but it also hurt my heart. There was a healing that needed to take place before I could move forward in Him and His plan. Although I learned tools and strategies from professionals on how to cope with my grief, I needed spiritual surgery that human doctors could not perform. I realized that God had to heal what was broken in my heart and He used the same thing that broke it in the first place: words. Have you ever been so angry with someone that you couldn't listen to reason or any argument they had and then out of nowhere they just apologized? The Scripture says that a soft or gentle answer deflects anger (Proverbs 15:1). When you hear a sincere apology, it deflates all the angry air out of your lungs. You lose the energy to continue to be fighting-mad. The words blow the red haze from around you and allow you to see the situation with clarity. You experience a change of heart because you realize that the person cares about you and the relationship you share with them. That's the first change that God did for me. He changed my heart.

The second definition is to change the mind of someone. Here is the second place God made changes in me. Although He healed my heart, I did a great deal of damage to my mind and my perception of my experience. Philippians 2:5 commands us to have the same mind or attitude that Jesus had. I was failing at this. My mind had conjured up that God should reward my faithfulness with a successful marriage and family. Then my mind spewed out thoughts of anger, bitterness and resentment when the marriage failed. My mind allowed the enemy to come in and plant depression and thoughts and plans of suicide. Those thoughts attacked my purpose and my passion. He had to rewire my mind and remind me that I'm His servant. He needed to heal the chemical damage the trauma of disappointment had caused. He changed my mind from thinking He didn't care about me by never leaving me alone in my rebellion. His love remained despite the hardness of my heart and the twisted thoughts of my mind. "For the mountains may move and the hills disappear, but even then, my faithful love for you will remain" (Isaiah 54:10 NLT).

The third definition is to renew a friendship. God's desire was to renew our friendship. God never stopped being my Friend; I stopped being His. He would tell me often that He missed the way I talked to Him. He missed the way I would share my day, my joys, my frustration, my love. I used to just say stuff out loud to Him as if He were right there in the flesh. As far as I was concerned, He was. He is Jehovah Shammah, the God that is always there and I talked to Him that way. When everything fell apart, I just stood with my arms folded in a defensive position with my back turned to Him. Please understand that I can fully comprehend just how dumb that was now, but at the time I could do nothing else. Yet He remained a true and faithful Friend to me and would constantly communicate with me His desire for me to return. I had returned, but with a different attitude than before. I returned because I knew it was the right thing to do. It was the safest thing to do. It was the only thing to do. I was glad to be back, but I wasn't fostering the same friendship as I had before. I wasn't seeing Him as a friend. I saw Him as my Creator. I saw Him as my Master. I saw Him as the One in charge and in control. I saw Him as Judge and the One who has the final say. I saw Him as my Forgiver, Healer, Provider. I wasn't, however, seeing Him as Friend. When I heard the apology, it brought to my attention just how much He had done and was still willing to do for me. It humbled me. It changed me. It changed my mind. It changed and renewed our friendship. I see Him differently than I ever did. Have I conquered every issue yet? Certainly not. What I do have an absolute clear understanding of is that God is a true friend. For that I am grateful.

So, I decided to accept His apology. I recognize that He doesn't owe me anything, but since He did apologize, I will accept. When I made that statement, I thought back to the definitions I studied about accepting His will for my life, so I decided to do the same with His apology. First, I approve of what He did, and I like that He did it. I like how He did it. I like what He said and the reason for what He said. I accept. Secondly, I surrender to His apology. I agree that our relationship needs to be restored. I give Him permission to do to me whatever it takes to put me back in right standing with Him. I yield to His commands, demands and persuasions. I accept. Third, I say yes to His invitation. He has invited me back into His will, His way, His word, His body, His love, His peace. He has invited me to operate in His anointing, through His power, under His authority. I accept. Next, I regard His apology to be true and sincere. I also believe in His forgiveness for me. Truth be told, I'm truly sorry for how I allowed everything to interfere with our relationship. I now embrace His judgment on the matter. I accept. Remember the fifth definition of accept? I receive His apology. I contain it in my heart, and I shape my heart to fit around His words. Those words spoken through His servant fit into all the holes that the enemy punctured in my soul. I have connectivity with God again because I accept.

I regard this God-given apology as more than suitable for the hurt I endured. I can regard our relationship as normal again because I accept. I move myself to stand under Him and what He speaks. I understand what He allowed was necessary for my purpose. I may not understand all the whys, but I understand He has a 'why' for it all. I accept. I take on the responsibility of what His apology means for my life. When God sends a word it continues for eternity. His apology is forever, and I now have a duty to never allow myself to fall prey to the enemy's tactic of allowing anything to come between Him and me. This task is monumental, but so is His apology. It is powerful enough to sustain me because it is His word. So, since He has laid this responsibility before me, I accept. I receive His apology without adverse reaction. His apology has done for me what Jehovah Raffa is known to do. It has healed. It is healing. It will continue to heal. The side effects of what He's allowed is no longer greater than the healing that has taken place. The side effects of what He's allowed is no longer greater than my destiny. The side effects of what He's allowed is no longer greater than my relationship with Him. My body is cooperating with the new transplant, and I no longer reject what God has allowed.

Finally, I reconcile myself with the Reconciler. I accommodate His presence in my life, and I make room for Him in my heart. I don't just save Him a room. I turn the keys to the whole house over to Him. I place myself back in the position of belonging to Him. I am His temple. I am His home. He has remodeled and redecorated me, and it suits me just fine. He is perfect. He is perfect in all His ways. I can only have perfection when I am in Him, so I place myself in Him.

Anyone who is angry with God, who is hurt by what He has allowed, who is devastated by what life has brought to them can only forgive Him when they get to this place. He has done nothing wrong and never will. He has not made a mistake and never will. There is not one flaw in Him and there never will be. Still I, and others like me, took offense. Now I must choose to undergo a change in my feelings and attitude. I must choose to shut down being resentful and bitter. I must choose to give Him my heart for His purpose. I must choose to give Him my life for His glory. I must choose to give Him my love for His pleasure. Give...for...For His purpose, glory, pleasure...I choose to give him my heart, my life, my love. I choose to for...give. How do you forgive a perfect God? You choose to forgive.

Epilogue

I realize that the choice to forgive God, or anyone, may be an extremely difficult one. This is especially true when the offense is so painful. This is where prayer comes in. Whenever we are faced with a task greater than our ability to complete, we should pray. In Luke 18:1, Jesus told a parable to His disciples to solidify the truth that we should always pray and never give up. When you are in the fight of your life, you may think it difficult to pray. Let me tell you this. Prayer is just a sincere desire of the heart. Prayer is an honest conversation with God. I found throughout this journey of being angry and unforgiving that I never stopped having honest conversations with God. Those conversations were sometimes rude, but they were always honest. I honestly told Him how I felt. I was truthful about my fears, my worries, my concerns.

He was also honest with me. He constantly reminded me of His love. He also reminded me of His sovereignty. As I said before, it was a conversation. Two beings who loved each other working through their relationship. My prayers weren't the kind you would hear inside a church during service. I didn't have fancy words of praise and flattery. I didn't use poetic phrases of petition. My prayers were raw. My words were sharp. We find prayers like this all throughout the Scriptures. Read through the Psalms, Job and the prophets. I sometimes wish we had every word of the prayers of Jesus in the garden. Even though we don't, it's still obvious that His praying was raw as well.

So, if this is the only way you can pray right now, don't worry. Just pray. Be honest. Be open. Have these tough conversations with God and work through your emotions. He won't leave you because you said the wrong thing; He didn't leave Job. He won't leave you because you sound depressed; He didn't leave Jeremiah. He won't leave you because you failed to do the right thing; He didn't leave David. He won't leave you because your words are full of anger; He didn't leave me. So let me help you get started.

Father God, in the name of Jesus I come to You. I come to you because I recognize Your sovereignty. I acknowledge your perfection. You are still who You are no matter how I feel or where my mind is.

I confess my anger, my confusion, my rebellion, my stubbornness and my hurt. I don't understand what You allowed in my life and my lack of understanding is causing a rift between us. I'm not sure I really want to talk to You, but I also know I would be devastated if You ever stopped talking to me. So here I am. I confess that I'm not ready to have this type of conversation with You, but my life is nothing without You. I'm desperate for a resolution, so I bow before You in submission. Forgive me.

Your Word says that You are a present help in trouble. I'm in trouble and I need help. I need help forgiving. I need help accepting. I need help in letting go of my anger. You are the only One who can do this. I don't really have much faith right now, but I have enough to ask You for help. It's hard to trust right now, but You've always been there for me even when I couldn't see You clearly. I know You're here right now. Help me to feel Your presence. Help me to discover or rediscover Your love.

Help me to be honest with You. Stop me from isolating myself. Give me strength to face You. Heal my heart and my mind. I open myself to Your Holy Spirit. Fill me, restore me and renew me. I don't want to live without You any longer. I embrace every word of correction. Change my attitude and my behavior.

I belong to You, and I always will. I surrender to Your plan for my life. I give You permission to allow what You deem necessary for me to fulfill Your purpose for my life. I thank You for never giving up on me. I thank You for reaching out to me. I thank You for Your lovingkindness and Your unfailing love. I pray all this in the name of Your Son, Jesus. Amen.

My hope for you is that you will continue to pray to God until you find the peace that He offers. God truly wants to be in communion with you and longs to have nothing separating your connection with Him. I pray that you find His joy because it will give you strength to continue the journey. Most of all, I long for you to know His absolute love. I say it as Paul said it in Romans 8:38-39 (NLT)...

And I am convinced that nothing can ever separate us from God's love. Neither death nor life, neither angels nor demons, neither our fears for today nor our worries about tomorrow--not even the powers of hell can separate us from God's love. No power in the sky above or in the earth below-- indeed, nothing in all creation will ever be able to separate us from the love of God that is revealed in Christ Jesus our Lord.

About the Author

 **La Tonya M. Daniels** was born in Elko, Nevada and raised in Las Vegas. She received her Bachelor's in music education from UNLV and her Master's in Administration and Supervision from University of Phoenix. She has also received two Advanced Studies Certificates through the Center for Teaching Excellence Program. She began teaching music in the Clark County School District in 1993. She retired from CCSD in 2021.

La Tonya has been gifted and talented since a young age. Using the gifts and talents God has blessed her with, she has served the community by performing at weddings, funerals, community events, and convalescent homes and has participated in spiritual and musical workshops as an instructor and coordinator. Her service to the Church of

God in Christ included local, district, and state levels. She has served at New Antioch Christian Fellowship in the Music, Kids Count (Children's Ministry), Servant Leader, Clerical, Creative Team, Greeter's, Community Outreach, Beauty Within, and Audio-Visual Ministries.

On January 20, 2008, she received her Ministerial ordination under the leadership of Pastor Naida M. Parson, PhD. Minister Daniels is called to preach, teach, evangelize and serve as a Levite for the House of God. She has a deep passion for children and their purpose and a love for the fine arts. As the meaning of her name states, she is a "Priceless Advisor" who shares wisdom through the arts to build better people.

Email: pricelessadvisor@gmail.com
Website: www.pricelessadvisor.org